AMERICAN PEASANT

AMERICAN PEASANT

by Christopher Schwarz

First published by Lost Art Press LLC in 2024
837 Willard St., Covington, KY 41011, USA
Web: http://lostartpress.com

Title: American Peasant
Author: Christopher Schwarz
Editor: Megan Fitzpatrick
Copy editor: Kara Gebhart Uhl
Distribution: John Hoffman
Project photos: Narayan Nayar

ISBN: 978-1-954697-19-5

First printing

This book was printed and bound in the United States.
Signature Book Printing, Inc.
http://signature-book.com

CONTENTS

FOREWORD

THE WOODEN-CLAD PAST

"Years ago I recognized my kinship with all living things, and I made up my mind that I was not one bit better than the meanest on earth... I say now, that while there is a lower class, I am in it; while there is a criminal element, I am of it; and while there is a soul in prison, I am not free."

— Eugene V. Debs (1855-1926), trade unionist, U.S. presidential candidate

I'm wasting the following two pages of pulp and ink because the subject matter of this book might seem odd for a woodworking text. This book deals with matters of religion, spirituality and magic. These are fascinating topics, but they are not what drew me to this work. Just like my book "Campaign Furniture" wasn't written from a love of empire, war or colonization.

For most of my career I have sought out aspects of the craft that have been ignored or nearly forgotten. If you are a woodworker in North America, it's easy to think that our craft begins with birdhouses, travels through the villages of the Shakers, tours the factories of the Arts & Crafts movement and ends somewhere with Midcentury Modern Furniture.

It's also easy to forget that for most of human civilization, the entire f-ing world was built from wood (plus some rocks and a few pieces of hardened metal). Most people's jobs dealt with wood, such as making crates or barrels, or traveling long distances on wooden boats and carriages. Other workers created everything else society needed by exploiting the tree, from paper to charcoal to chewing gum.

Every culture that was surrounded by trees used them to create a different furniture tradition. And many of these civilizations are invisible to Western woodworkers.

Whenever I travel abroad or simply visit the British Museum (cultural repository of ransackers extraordinaire), I am dumbstruck by the diversity of woodwork across time and space. Westerners – myself included – have seen only a glimpse of the beautiful ways that people have split, shaped and adorned wood to fulfill a basic need or honor a higher power.

If our myopic view of the craft is ever going to change, then we will need a lot more woodworkers. And so I present my "want ad" for everyone and anyone to join the search.

Clears throat. Speaks in the deep voice of Klaatu from "The Day the Earth Stood Still." Or Morgan Freeman. Or… damn it, whatever voice you have.

The craft of woodworking is not a religion. The craft does not care if you use dirty words or pious ones. There are no prayers that are part of the craft. There are no spiritual requirements to become proficient at it. You will not be a better woodworker if you use fewer (or more) cuss words or keep your pants on in the gardening aisle at Walmart. You can be a craven criminal, a priest or both and still be an outstanding or pathetic woodworker.

I've read enough accounts of historical shops to know that the workshops of the past were just like the shops of today. They were filled with pious people and ribald ones. Drunkards and sober individuals. Predators and decent human beings. Just like the place you work right now.

The craft is not a self-help group. It has become common today for some individuals to associate the craft with therapy or spirituality or a connection to a nature goddess. These associations do not come from the craft. Instead, they have been grafted onto the craft by people with an agenda (maybe good; maybe not).

We might experience emotions or feelings in our bodies as we perform the craft. But the craft doesn't create these emotions. We do. And the craft does not give a single crap about our feelings.

The craft is bigger than all of that.

So then, what does the craft demand? 1) An understanding of its essential tools, materials and processes; 2) a commitment to repeating them until they are internalized and performed competently; and 3) a level of competence that allows its knowledge and skills to be taught to others.

And no more.

The craft welcomes you. And it begs you to find your place in it. To unearth a little bit of its history, embrace it and share it with others before we are drowned in a sea of plastic and petroleum by-products.

Wood everywhere. The building. The walls. The rack, spoons and plates.

This book is not a religious screed, instruction book or self-help text. Instead, "American Peasant" is (I hope) a sound attempt to shine a light on some beautiful objects produced in Scandinavia, and Eastern and Central Europe, and to perhaps forge some small connection between these items and the stories my paternal grandfather told me about our family's journey from Ukraine to the U.S.

In some small way, I hope it might inspire you to embark on your own journey through our wooden-clad past.

Christopher Schwarz
Covington, Kentucky
January 2024

CHAPTER 1

SOME LOVELY FILTH DOWN 'ERE

You must discard the word Fancy altogether. You have nothing to do with it. You are not to have, in any object of use or ornament, what would be a contradiction in fact. You don't walk upon flowers in fact; you cannot be allowed to walk upon flowers in carpets. You don't find that foreign birds and butterflies come and perch upon your crockery; you cannot be permitted to paint foreign birds and butterflies upon your crockery. You never meet with quadrupeds going up and down walls; you must not have quadrupeds represented upon walls. 'You must use,' said the gentleman, 'for all these purposes, combinations and modifications (in primary colours) of mathematical figures which are susceptible of proof and demonstration. This is the new discovery. This is fact. This is taste.'

— Thomas Gradgrind in "Hard Times," Charles Dickens, 1854

I'm no tenant farmer. I didn't grow up in a feudal system where my family had to forfeit a large part of our harvest to a petty lord or bishop. In fact, I have never farmed a single day in my damn life.

So, the title of this book, "American Peasant," might seem a puzzle (at the least) or even a bit deceptive.

Of course, there are many ways to interpret the word "peasant." First, let me say that I don't consider the term derogatory. In fact, the primary goal of this book is to open a few eyes to the gorgeous peasant furniture forms that get little attention in the West. And to perhaps shift the West's understanding of what a peasant was (or is).

I would be happy for you to interpret the title as: "American Peasant: Hello America, I'd Like You to Meet Some Peasants."

It's an introduction that is overdue.

I have spent my life studying furniture and amassing a library of books about woodworking. Yet, until Peter Follansbee introduced me to the work of Hungarian woodworker Gyenes Tamás in 2015, I'd never seen anything like these peasant pieces. And I mean that sentence literally: These pieces were foreign in form, construction, finish and embellishment.

To fill that void, I first made a rough translation of Tamás' book, "Ácsolt ládák titkai." And I found my way into the ethnographic studies of so-called "peasant art" in Northern, Eastern and Central Europe.

I started building these furniture pieces as best I could. I developed engraving tools (by MacGyvering aluminum craft knives and cheap vinyl flooring cutters) to mimic the beautiful engravings. I buckled down and learned to use straight-up linseed oil paint, which is a joy.

And – this is big – I embraced embellishment.

For my entire furniture-making career, I have been but mildly interested in carving, marquetry, parquetry, stringing and inlay. Instead, I have always focused on form, grain and form. Plus grain. And form.

Suddenly I wanted to engrave the outline of a farmer kneeling in prayer on every door I made. Plowed fields on my joined chests. Plus mountains covered in evergreens that were protected by unseen forces. I had ingested someone's cabbage-flavored Kool-Aid.

Traditional European peasant culture has virtually disappeared outside of old books and far-flung museums. And it's difficult for a modern Westerner to even conceive of just how different the society and material culture was in Eastern and Central Europe. Peasants are almost a trope in the West, thanks in no small part to "Monty Python and the Holy Grail." Impossibly poor, dirty and hopeless people. ("Dennis, there's some lovely filth down 'ere.")

But when you see the early photos of peasant homes, clothes and decorative objects, it's humbling. These rural societies were complex, skilled, fastidious and proud. Peasant homes, churches and granaries are wonders of construction, human-scale, made from good materials and (when you see the interiors) a place you would love to spend a long evening. Or a lifetime.

Everyday objects, from the shepherd's crook to the grain scoop, were embellished. Not with gold or rubies. But with the skill of the axe and the knife.

These entire societies were built on wood. And yet, most woodworkers outside those isolated countries have no clue that these wondrous places and objects even existed.

As I page through the old books that document the life of European peasants, I am both awed and saddened. This physical world doesn't exist anymore, except in museums and memories. We have traded it for a plastic society

Grave markers, Transylvania.

with cheap clothes and stamped metal silverware. To be sure, some things are better now. The medicine. The rights of women and minorities. But when it comes to material objects, modern culture is in retrograde.

This book is a brief glimpse at some of my favorite peasant forms and the low-relief engravings that cover them. I attempted to make the furniture in the same spirit as the originals, with traditional joinery, animal glue and linseed oil paint. But I also tried to make the projects approachable for the home woodworker in the West. (My biggest compromise was using sawn boards instead of rived ones.)

So, a second way to read the title of this book is: "American Peasant: Here are Some Peasant Pieces Lightly Adapted for American Woodworkers."

There is a third aspect to this book's title that might not be immediately obvious. And that is what the word "peasant" means to me. Or – perhaps more important – what it doesn't mean. Peasants aren't wealthy. They're powerless. They might not own land. And they're not particularly valued by high society.

Yet, their work endures. And if you can find it, you'll see that one thing is clear: Their furniture and decorative objects are – for the most part – indifferent to the furniture traditions of the wealthy and the powerful.

This is an important point. Too often, rural styles of furniture are explained as less-sophisticated echoes of what the elite had in their homes. The story goes something like: A peasant doing work in the manor house spies a high-style Louis XIV chair. Then sneaks back to the cottage to make a version from animal bones and dung.

Which is – sorry – utter bullshit.

In many cases vernacular forms have no equivalent to the pieces in the drawing rooms or dressing chambers of the powdered gouters. Is there a high-style version of the dry sink, the tater bin, the mule chest, the creepie or the plate rack? Do the royalty have elaborately carved bacon settles or chicken coops integrated with their kitchen cabinetry? No.

But it's not just the forms that are different. The symbolism on the furniture is different, too.

The wealthy in the West prefer vicious raptors, arrows, shields, olive branches and (of course) all the Roman and Greek stuff that reinforces their elite status. The message is clear: This piece is owned by someone powerful. He could crush you. But if you're nice, you might get an olive branch (instead of an arrow in your ass).

The symbology on peasant pieces is more humane: Please protect our loved ones. Keep our fields from harm. Hey, I'd like you to meet my family. I wish you eternal love. And do not waste the short time you have on earth.

So even though I have never plowed a single field, I have thrown my lot in with the peasants of the world.

What does that mean? I have spent most of my adult life working for myself, and I resent (sometimes deeply) wealth and privilege. Instead, the center of my life is my family, community and our material culture. I love simple rituals, like our Friday evening walks to our local bar where we share a glass of wine and recount the work of the week with the other shopkeepers. Or the Sunday evening meals with my extended family. And the eating of the pizza on every Wednesday (a high holy day).

I have taught my children to look their friends deep in the eye when they raise a glass to toast an important event, or just a good meal. They know to say "rabbit, rabbit, rabbit" immediately when they wake up on the first day of each month. Food is our currency, and some of our family rituals are too complex and odd to explain.

And because we've never had a lot of it, money isn't all that important. I work hard enough to own a small Toyota pickup truck and a nice set of tools. Because I build chairs on Sundays and sell them, we can afford some good food, plus the occasional trip (tacked on to the end of a teaching assignment). We barter and exchange favors with our friends and neighbors when we can. We fix (for free) the drawers, chests, shelves and picture frames of anyone in our neighborhood who comes through the door. And in exchange we find cinnamon rolls on our doorstep or a shoveled walk after a heavy snow.

All I want out of this life is some good work – to exercise my body and

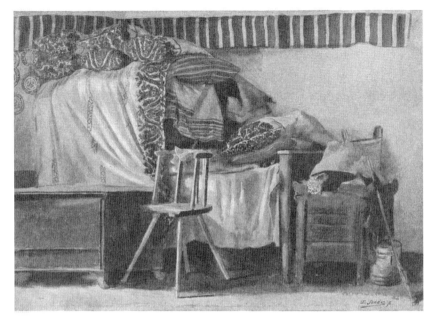

Peasant home interior from "Peasant Art in Sweden, Lapland and Iceland" (The Studio, 1910).

my mind every day and make beautiful things. I want to protect my family, friends and this particular way of living. And I want to help as many people as I can – friends, strangers and all.

I don't know what to call this life exactly, but for many years I have felt like I'm an American peasant.

CHAPTER 2

THE PEASANT'S WORKSHOP

You don't need a dedicated workshop – or even a workbench – to build furniture. I constructed my first dozen pieces of furniture on the floor of our back porch in Lexington, Kentucky. And when I needed to perform an operation up off the ground, I used our kitchen table.

I don't recall wanting a workbench until someone told me I needed one.

A dedicated workshop is a significant investment in space, and usually money. If you are just getting started in woodworking or live in a tiny space, here's how you can do many hand-tool operations with a kitchen table (or a picnic table), plus some scraps of wood and a few clamps.

And though the photos in this chapter are obviously staged for this book, this is how I worked for years in our Lexington home. And I have used these methods when working on-site, or at woodworking schools with inadequate workbenches. They really work.

ABOUT THAT TABLE

Almost any kitchen table will do if you are brave enough. A table with a 1-1/2"-thick top is ideal. It won't flex or move much while you handplane your parts. If you do find that your table scoots too much, screw cleats to the floor to immobilize its legs. If you're cringing, maybe take up golf instead. A few screw holes in the floor are easy to fill when your lease expires.

Most kitchen tables are flat enough for woodworking chores. If the table does have a low spot that prevents your planes from working (you'll quickly realize the problem), here's a solution: Cover the table with a piece of 3/4"

MDF while you are using the table for woodworking. MDF is heavy and flat. Your lumberyard or home center will gladly cut it to size for you.

Another possible solution is to use a kitchen countertop as a workbench. I've done this in a pinch while on the road. Kitchen countertops are great because they are already screwed to the floor and walls. But countertops usually overhang the cabinets below only about 1-1/4" or 1-1/2". And that's not a lot of space for clamps to do their job.

I've had more luck using a kitchen island, however. Especially when part of the island was dedicated to seating and dining and there was some empty space below the countertop where I could maneuver some clamps.

SAWING STUFF TO SIZE
To crosscut boards, clamp them to your tabletop with the waste hanging off the edge. If the board is too long for the room or the table, do the job on top of 5-gallon buckets on the ground (thanks to Mike Siemsen for this tip). Here's how: Turn the buckets upside down on the floor. Place the board on the buckets with the waste hanging off (or support the waste from below with a third 5-gallon bucket).

Use one knee to hold the board in place on a bucket as you crosscut the board to length.

To rip boards along their length, forget the buckets. Instead, clamp the board to your kitchen table with the waste hanging off the tabletop. Rip while standing up – it's called "overhand ripping." It's easier on your back and requires less energy. (Or get a small band saw, which I discuss below.)

To saw small stuff, make some bench hooks. You'll use these hooks for the rest of your life – even if you build a nice workbench someday. I have several of these hooks that I've made during the last 25 years in different sizes – all made from scraps.

PLANE THE FACES OF BOARDS
To plane the faces of boards, clamp a strip of wood that is thinner than the stock you are planing to the end of the table. For example, if you are planing 3/4" stock, your planing stop should be 1/2" thick or less. Keep a few of these planing stops sitting around in various thicknesses – 1/4" and 1/2" should handle most chores. For planing even thinner stock, clamp a yardstick to the end of the bench to act as a planing stop.

Likewise, if you are using a picnic table as a workbench, screws and nails are your friends for most things. You can fasten stops anywhere you like on the picnic table. You can, in fact, simply drive two or three screws into the tabletop to act as height-adjustable planing stops.

Even the lightest of tables on the slickest of floors can be immobilized with a few fasteners and/
or blocks of wood.

Overhand ripping at a table or workbench is a good skill to learn, especially if you don't enjoy
bending over sawhorses.

This improved bench hook/shooting board ensures your saw won't scar your dining table. The underside (shown above) acts as a bench hook. Flip it over (below) and it's a shooting board. The whole thing is made of 1/2" plywood that is glued and nailed together.

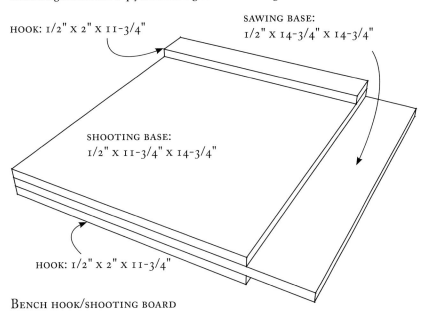

HOOK: 1/2" X 2" X 11-3/4"

SAWING BASE: 1/2" X 14-3/4" X 14-3/4"

SHOOTING BASE: 1/2" X 11-3/4" X 14-3/4"

HOOK: 1/2" X 2" X 11-3/4"

BENCH HOOK/SHOOTING BOARD

A scrap piece of plywood (1/2" in this case) and some small F-style clamps from the hardware store make an effective planing stop.

PLANE THE LONG EDGES

To plane the long edges of boards, use one of two strategies. For narrow boards (about 2" to 3" wide) simply butt them against your planing stop and get to work. The weight of the tool and the forward force of pushing the tool will hold the work in place.

For wider boards, clamp a handscrew to the end of the tabletop. Use the handscrew to pinch one end of the board. Plane toward the handscrew.

PLANE THE ENDS OF BOARDS

This is sometimes called "shooting." It can be done with a special appliance called a "shooting board." Or you can just wing it (which is what I do most of the time). If you don't have a bench vise to hold the board steady, clamp a pair of handscrews to the workbench to grab the long edges of the board. Then plane the end of the board straight and clean.

You will quickly learn about "spelching," which is when you break off a corner of the board. I avoid spelching by planing a small chamfer on the far end of the board. Or by planing from each end of the board and toward the middle of the board.

[11]

A handscrew clamped to the corner of your dining table is an effective vise for holding boards on edge while planing them.

Two handscrews clamped to your table make an effective vise for planing end grain or even sawing dovetails.

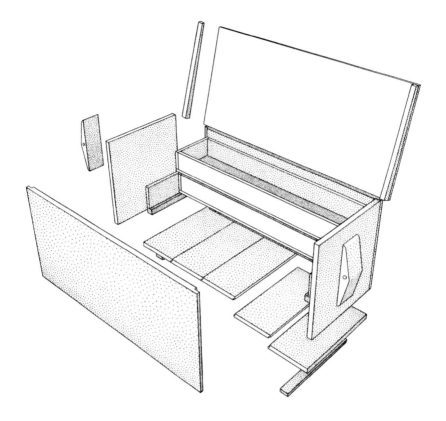

A simple nailed-together tool chest with sliding tills (also nailed together) is enough to serve most woodworkers for a lifetime.

JOINERY

Most of the joinery in this book is dados, rabbets and nails – plus some grooves and mortise-and-tenon joinery. You will have no problem clamping your work to the table to cut these joints with a rabbet plane, chisels and saws. And maybe a bench hook.

THE PEASANT'S TOOL CHEST

I considered building a tool chest specifically for this book. Then I realized that I could not improve upon the simple boarded tool chest I built for "The Anarchist's Design Book." I still use that chest every day, and it has held up great. It is just rabbets, glue and nails. I have included it as an appendix at the end of this book.

WHAT TO PUT IN THE CHEST

The following tools are what I think are necessary to build the projects in this book. There are many ways to do many operations, so these aren't gospel.

Primary Tools
Jack plane. I prefer a vintage Stanley No. 5 ground with a curved iron.
Block plane
No. 48 tonguing and grooving plane. (Details are in a separate chapter.)
Cutting gauge
Mallet
1/2" and 3/4" chisel
2" chisel
Tenon saw
Carcase saw
16-ounce nail hammer. I prefer a wooden handle.
Hand drill and brace (or battery-powered drill)
Handsaw, 7 points per inch
Ripsaw, 6-7 points per inch
Marking knife
12" combination square
Coping saw
Cabinet rasp
Card scraper
Augers and brad-point bits
Engraving tool. (Details are in a separate chapter.)
6" pencil compass
1/4" and 5/16" mortise chisel
Cork sanding block

Optional Tools
Scorp or drawknife
Shoulder plane or rabbet plane
Beading plane (1/8")
Froe
Hatchet
Router plane

CONSIDER ONE MACHINE

If you want to reduce the time it takes to build these projects by half, I recommend buying a little 10" benchtop band saw. Most come with a half-decent fence. Add a quality 5/16"-wide blade, and the saw will save you significant time and labor.

These machines are not particularly noisy – about as loud as a sewing machine. They have more than enough power to cut domestic hardwoods up to 2" thick (yes, I was surprised by this fact as well). And most of them have better dust collection than the big band saws. Mine hooks right to my shop vacuum and leaves little dust behind.

Plus, you can put it in a closet when you are done working.

The downsides to a small band saw are not significant for a home wood-worker. Yes, some of the components are aluminum or plastic – instead of iron or steel. And the machine's wheels are a little lightweight. These saws aren't designed to be flogged like a rented mule for eight hours a day with a lot of heavy rips and resawing.

If you are using a band saw on nights and weekends, these downsides will never make themselves apparent.

WHAT'S AT HAND

Don't put off building a project because you don't have this, that or the other. Roy Underhill cut his first dovetails by holding the boards against some steps with his foot. Many professional woodworkers have workbenches that are nothing more than sawhorses and a door.

What you need is a small place to work. What you don't need are excuses.

CHAPTER 3

ON WOOD & JOINERY

Wood has always been a valuable commodity, and it can be hard to come by the good stuff you need to make furniture. So, when you are faced with choosing wood for the projects in this book, I suggest you take a cue from the peasants of Central and Eastern Europe: Use whatever is available. And use it to the fullest.

For a Carpathian peasant, that might be beech boards that must be rived, then shaped with a drawknife. A Romanian shepherd might look for a crooked stick to make an inlaid staff. Or they might find oak, birch or pine in the forest.

In North America, you are unlikely to find lots of beech or birch. But you can easily find tulip poplar (which is actually a magnolia – not the garbage ornamental tree). Or red oak. Pine of one sort or another is everywhere.

There are no particular magical properties to the species used for this sort of furniture. What's most important is that you can shape it with the tools you have on hand, and that it's dry enough to assemble into furniture.

If you are going to use wet wood – what we call "green wood" right from the living tree – then you need to learn to cut, split and dry your parts. It's a satisfying process, but it has a learning curve and requires some space outdoors so you can make a mess with the bark and the random splits. Plus, you need room to dry the wood outside, then finish the process in your shop.

Because I live in the inner city and have no green space, I buy sawn boards from the lumberyard. If I pick stock that has dead-straight grain, I can split it out with a froe and a mallet, which I did for many of the pieces in this book.

Oak, ash and poplar split easily, even when kiln-dried. In fact, many times I choose to split it out because splitting is faster than handsawing. Splitting wood is sometimes even faster than ripping boards with a band saw.

After splitting it out, I clean up the pieces with a drawknife then a jack plane. It's messy and time-consuming, but satisfying. If you have the material and the space, I recommend it.

But that's neither the only way nor the "right" way to approach these projects.

A handful of small machines, such as a 10" band saw, allow you to use boards from the lumberyard to make these projects. These small and sturdy machines cost less than a premium handplane, but they can save hours of ripping or scrollwork with hand-powered saws.

I slide easily between machines and hand tools, and I don't consider the choice between them to be mutually exclusive. Use what you have. Or, barring that, use what you enjoy. Or, barring that, do what I do: Use what will keep food on your table and your work in demand.

TIPS FOR SELECTING STOCK

Many of these projects are engraved with spells or symbols, so you need to take care when picking your stock. If you rive your boards, the process ensures the grain in the board runs straight through the stock. Engraving these boards is a breeze.

If you purchase sawn boards, however, you have no guarantee about the grain. The saw at the mill is happy to produce boards with grain that is angled dramatically through the thickness of the stock.

Engraving boards that have a dramatic grain direction is possible but difficult. You need to take light passes when engraving against the grain.

The better course is to look for boards at the lumberyard that have long sections where the grain runs straight through the thickness of the board.

It's rare to find a board where the grain is dead-straight throughout the board's entire length. I'm happy if the board has straight grain through two-thirds of the board. I save the straight sections for a piece that will be engraved. And I use the sections with angled grain for parts that won't get engraved, such as the bottoms of chests and the backboards of shelving.

GOOD SPECIES FOR ENGRAVING

When I started working with engraving tools, I suspected that the species that are ideal for carving, such as basswood, would be the best for engraving, too. Basswood is indeed easy to engrave – as long as the grain runs straight through the thickness of the board.

After engraving thousands of lines and arcs, here are some suggestions:

1. Straight grain, especially in quartersawn woods, is the easiest to engrave.

You can split kiln-dried wood. I've done it for years. The froe will show you how the grain is running through diffuse-porous boards, such as this poplar.

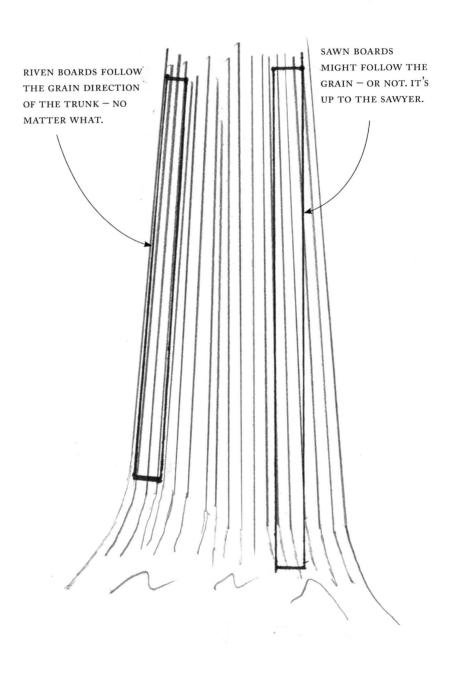

RIVEN BOARDS FOLLOW
THE GRAIN DIRECTION
OF THE TRUNK — NO
MATTER WHAT.

SAWN BOARDS
MIGHT FOLLOW THE
GRAIN — OR NOT. IT'S
UP TO THE SAWYER.

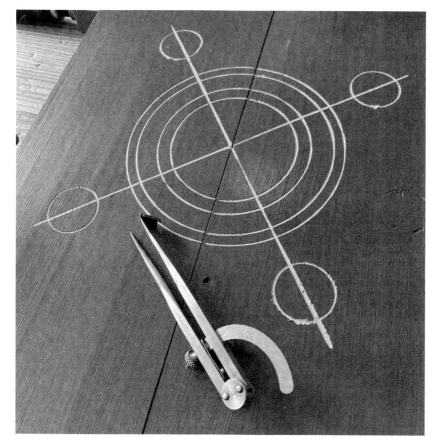

Dead-straight grain is ideal for joinery and for engraving.

2. A sharp engraving cutter can handle most woods, including oak and ash.

3. When you begin an engraving, sharpen the cutter, then make a few practice cuts in the species you are about to engrave. Getting warmed up is never a waste of time.

The engraving tools make a shallow cut – 1/16" deep at most – so only the hardest woods put up a fight. With a sharp cutter, engraving cherry, walnut, maple, beech, birch and oak is easy.

The soft woods, especially the soft-as-wet-toilet-paper pines – can be difficult to engrave. Your cutter must be keen, otherwise the soft fibers get crushed, and they look like a booger from space has impacted your project.

[21]

NOTES ON JOINERY

The joinery in these projects is, for the most part, standard stuff. Lots of mortise-and-tenon joints, plus nails and tongue-and-groove joints.

However, one of the joints for making panels deserves special mention. When making a panel from several boards for the lid or front of a carcase, the individual pieces are shaped differently.

Instead of being flat boards, the pieces are triangular in cross section. This shape is the result of the board being rived from a round tree. (Think of each board as a piece of pie.) Instead of flattening these boards, the peasant woodworkers would use the triangular shape to their advantage.

The thin tip of the pie piece would become the tongue. Then the thick end would get grooved. The assembled panel looks like a bunch of shingles intersecting each other.

If you rive out your boards, this sort of joinery makes sense. But if you start with flat boards, it does not. For the Large Coffer, I tried imitating this construction by surfacing my boards by hand so they were triangular in cross section. It was a lot of work.

If you do want to explore this traditional method of joinery, I recommend you seek out the work of Hungarian woodworker Gyenes Tamás and his book "Ácsolt ládák titkai" (self published).

Mostly, I encourage you to use the woods around you. Learn all you can about the trees in your town, no matter if they are junk trees or ornamentals. You can make furniture using almost any wood out there. Our ancestors certainly did. The only thing stopping you is some doofus who says that dogwood isn't worth shit.

But it is. You can make daggers out of it. Or drawbore pegs. Or spoons.

RIVEN PANELS TEND TO BE TRIANGULAR IN
CROSS SECTION.

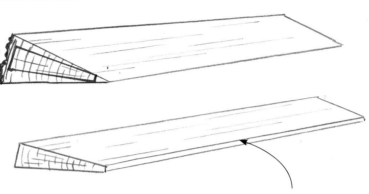

REMOVE THE PITH TO CREATE THE TONGUE.
THEN SHAVE THE EXCESS THICKNESS.

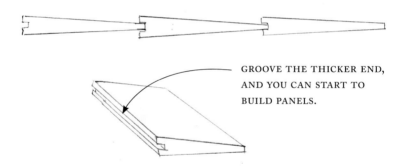

GROOVE THE THICKER END,
AND YOU CAN START TO
BUILD PANELS.

CHAPTER 4

TONGUE & GROOVE PLANES

Many projects in this book use a tongue-and-groove joint to create the wide panels that make up the fronts, sides, backs, lids and bottoms of the pieces.

On many original pieces in Eastern Europe, this joint was created using rived stock, as discussed in the previous chapter. The tongue was at the tip of the board. The groove was plowed with a T-shaped grooving tool that is unavailable in the West. It's a clever and effective way to build furniture – if you have rived stock.

Sawn stock from the lumberyard or mill is rectangular in cross section. And the grain is rarely dead straight through the board. So the approach to making these pieces requires a different tool.

For centuries, planemakers have made wooden-bodied tongue-and-groove planes, sometimes called "match planes." One plane makes the tongue; a second makes the matching groove. These tools are effective, if you can find them in working order and they haven't lost their mate.

Stanley Works had a clever solution. In 1875, Stanley started making the No. 48 Tonguing and Grooving Plane. It is one plane that makes both parts of the joint. The position of the tool's rotating fence determines which part of the joint the plane cuts.

In one position, the fence exposes only one of the plane's two cutters to the wood. So it makes a groove. Spin the fence 180°, and it exposes two cutters, which makes the tongue.

The No. 48 was designed to be used on stock from 3/4" to 1-1/4" in thick-

TONGUING AND GROOVING PLANE.

PATENTED.

The stock of this tool is made of metal, and it has two cutters fastened into the stock by thumb screws. The guide, or fence, when set as shown in the above engraving, allows both of the cutters to act ; and the cutters being placed at a suitable distance apart, a perfect Tonguing Plane is made. The guide, or fence, which is hung on a pivot at its centre, may be easily swung around, end for end ; thus one of the cutters will be covered, and the guide held in a new position, thereby converting the Tool into a Grooving Plane A groove will be cut to exactly match the tongue which is made by the other adjustment of the Tool

The ingenuity and simplicity of this Tool, together with its compact form and durability, will commend it to the favorable regard of all wood-working mechanics.

PRICE, including Tonguing and Grooving Tools.

No. 48.   Iron Stock and Fence, for $\frac{3}{4}$ to $1\frac{1}{4}$ inch Boards......$2 50

No. 49.   Iron Stock and Fence, for $\frac{3}{8}$ to $\frac{3}{4}$ inch Boards....... 2 50

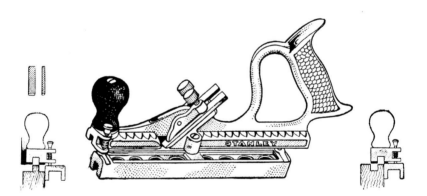

Vintage Stanley catalog listings for its tonguing and grooving plane.

A Stanley No. 48 set up for tonguing (left) and grooving (right).

ness, with the tongue centered on 7/8"-thick stock. Later, Stanley made a smaller plane, the No. 49, which joins boards that are 1/2" thick (though it could handle boards that were slightly thinner and thicker).

The Nos. 48 and 49 are remarkable tools, and Stanley made many of them. So you can find them (and copies of them) on the used market. Sometimes their irons go missing, but replacements are out there or can be made easily.

Lie-Nielsen Toolworks makes heavy-duty versions of the Nos. 48 and 49, which have some improvements, especially the tools' wooden handles and the use of a single iron, instead of two irons. These are the tools I use throughout this book, and I recommend them. (Note: There are other modern manufacturers who make planes that can do the same task, but you must swap out some tooling to make both parts of the joint.)

Both the Stanley and Lie-Nielsen tools have some peculiarities in setting them up and using them. Here are some tips to get you started.

SHARPENING

I sharpen almost all my plane blades at 35°. This keeps my life simple, and it doesn't hurt how the tools perform. Argue the minutiae with me over a beer sometime, but the simple fact is that this is how I have worked for many years.

To ensure my edges are dead-square and at 35°, I use a side-clamping honing guide when possible.

To sharpen the two blades for the Stanley versions of these planes, you clamp them in the honing guide and sharpen them like a bench chisel.

The ingenious Lie-Nielsen forked cutter clamped (with care) in a honing guide.

If you own a Lie-Nielsen version of this tool, you have only one iron to sharpen, which looks like a forked tongue. You can sharpen this iron in a honing guide, but you need to be careful when cinching down the guide on the blade. With some honing guides, you can bend the forks of this blade. So take care and cinch the guide down to where the blade is held firm, but isn't bending.

SETUP

Setting up the Lie-Nielsen tools is simple. Put the forked blade in the tool, secure the lever cap and set the blade projection. Set it for as heavy a cut as your muscles can manage.

Setting the blades for the original Stanleys takes more fiddling, but that is a positive aspect of this plane. I set the blade that is farthest from the fence a little deeper than the blade near the fence. These slightly offset cutters ensure tight-fitting joints. Here's how:

First thing to know: The fence of the tool should always run against the "true surface" of every board. This is true for both the tongue and the groove.

If the term "true surface" boggles you, here's a quick explanation. In handwork, we call a surface "true" if it has been flattened so it can join other surfaces. On a dining table, for example, the underside of the tabletop needs to

[28]

TRUE FACES OF
BOARDS. THE FENCE
OF THE PLANE RUNS
AGAINST THESE FACES.

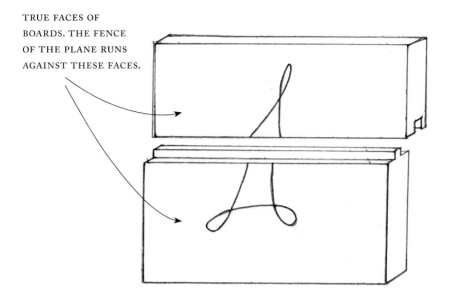

The true face relates to other pieces of the project. The true face of a tabletop is the underside because it has to mate with the base.

be true so it sits flat on the table's base. The top surface just has to look flat. So when you are tonguing and grooving backboards for a cabinet, the fence needs to ride against the faces of the boards that will face toward the inside of the cabinet.

So, when the single cutter is exposed to make the groove, the groove is a little deeper than normal because the blade is set deeper.

When set to make the tongue, the deeper cutter overcuts a little compared to its shy cousin. The net result: The show surface of the joint is always tight. The non-show surface has a small gap between the boards.

USE

The main difficulty with these tools is that the fence becomes wobbly. This is almost always caused by the user "unscrewing" the fence as they switch back and forth between the tonguing and grooving settings. If the fence becomes too loose, the boards won't mate flush.

I keep a screwdriver on the bench when I use these planes. And I make sure the tip of the screwdriver fits the head of the screw on which the fence pivots (this prevents the screw's slot from getting chewed up). After I adjust the fence, I snug up the screw, which prevents the fence from wiggling.

ONE BLADE IS SET DEEPER
THAN THE OTHER BLADE.

THIS
CREATES AN
INTENTIONAL
GAP ON THE
BACKSIDE OF
THE JOINT. THE
FACE OF THE
JOINT IS TIGHT.

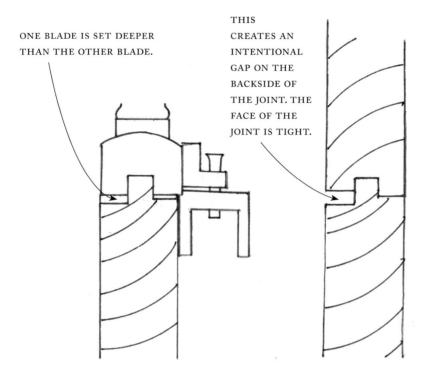

One of the advantages of separate blades is that you can set one deeper than the other – ensuring a gap on the back and a tight joint facing the user.

Whenever I spin the fence on my tongue-and-groove plane, I cinch the center screw to keep everything tight.

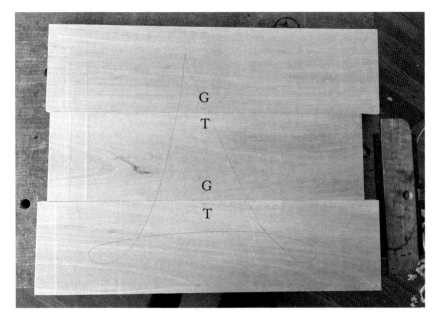

A cabinetmaker's triangle and some T and G marks guide my work when making a panel.

LAY OUT THE PANEL

Arrange the pieces on your workbench to create the desired panel. I usually put the heart side facing up (if the wood is dry). If it's damp, I'll alternate heart side and bark side on each mating board to decrease the chance the panel will distort as it comes into equilibrium with the humidity level in my shop.

I orient the boards so the grain direction on all the boards is running left (if you are left-handed, reverse this and have the grain running to the right). This ensures the No. 48 will be (mostly) working with the grain during the whole process.

To be fair, a little tear-out on the edges of the tongues or the grooves isn't a big deal. The tearing will be mostly hidden. But in boards that have the grain moving steeply through the board, the tearing can show on the face of the board. Plus, working against the grain is harder work.

Now draw a giant and bold cabinetmaker's triangle across all the boards. Decide which edges will get a tongue and which will get a groove. Mark a T or a G near that edge to remind you.

Place the first board in your face vise with the edge that will be tongued facing up. The cabinetmaker's triangle should face you, the user. If the fence of the No. 48 runs against the triangle-marked surface on all the boards, then the panel will end up flat with the surfaces coplanar.

[31]

Work with the grain when possible. But when you cannot, don't worry too much about tear-out on the inside of the joint.

Joint the board's edge and check to make sure it is true. This is not as finicky a process as jointing an edge for glue-up. You just want to make the edge clean and mostly straight.

Take the No. 48 and set its blades for a rank cut – so rank it makes a stank (I don't know what that means, but it rhymes and so I like it). In the photos shown here, my shaving is 0.025" thick. (That's 12 to 25 times as thick as a shaving from a smooth plane.) Basically, take the thickest shaving you can manage that leaves a (mostly) clean surface behind.

Set the swinging fence of the No. 48 so it makes a tongue. The fence should be snug and not wobbly. If it wobbles, the plane will wander and the pieces won't go together well. If the fence is a little loose, snug it up with a screwdriver. As soon as the fence stops its wobble, stop tightening the screw. It's easy to over-tighten.

Place the No. 48 on the board's edge. Your dominant hand holds the tote just like any plane. But the off-hand does something else. Don't grab the front

This is no time for wispy shavings. Hog off the thickest curls you can manage.

knob. Otherwise, the plane is more likely to tilt and break off the tongue or groove as you work.

Place the thumb of your off-hand on the plane's body behind the front knob. Tuck your fingers under the fence and into the groove in the No. 48's fence. Use your fingers to press the fence against the work.

Now cut the tongue. Use your body as much as your arms to move the plane. When the plane stops cutting, remove it from the board. With your jack plane, chamfer simultaneously both the corner of the board and the corner of the tongue. Four or five strokes should do it. The chamfers hide small imperfections and make it easy to assemble the panel.

Tip: Keep an oily rag (my preference) or chunk of paraffin wax handy as you work. After I complete every joint, I wipe the fence and the sole of the tool with the oily rag. This makes a huge difference in how easy the tool is to push.

The pause to wipe also allows me to double-check the next board in my pile to ensure it's oriented correctly as I put it in the vise. It's easy to get turned around as you work and start making fatal errors.

A few strokes with a jack plane can ease assembly and make everything look tidy.

MAKE THE GROOVE

If there's a groove on the board's opposite edge, flip the board in the vise end-over-end so the cabinetmaker's triangle always faces you. Joint the board's edge. Set the No. 48 to cut a groove. Check for fence wobble and tighten it if necessary.

Place the plane on the edge and plow the groove. When the groove is complete, chamfer the corners of this edge, too.

CLEANUP

Take the board out of the vise and jam its end against your planing stop. Clean off the true face of the board with a jack plane, removing the cabinetmaker's triangle. With the jack set for a rank cut, it's easy to leave weird little ripple marks at the beginning of the cut as you start the plane. To avoid them, skew the plane at the beginning of the cut and straighten out the tool over about 12" of movement.

Flip the board end-over-end and plane the underside of the board. Flip the board end-over-end again and place the finished board in position with its mating boards. Be careful: With the triangle removed it's easy to get turned around. I sometimes affix a piece of blue tape to the faces of the boards that face up.

[34]

When gluing up a tongue-and-groove panel simply brush glue in the groove and assemble the bits. Then clamp.

Plane the rest of the boards to make their tongues and grooves. And plane their faces. When all the boards in the panel are complete, glue up the panel with bar clamps.

First disassemble the parts and arrange all the boards so their grooves face up and lean against the clamp heads. You can then paint glue into all the grooves simultaneously as you work your way down the edges with a glue bottle and brush.

Pull the boards together using hand pressure. Not a mallet. Place one clamp across the middle of the panel with its bar on top of the panel. The other clamp bars can go below the panel. The middle clamp prevents the panel from springing up and out of the clamps.

Apply clamp pressure in the middle of the board. Work your way out to the ends. The joints on the boards' edges keep everything in line, so glue-up isn't stressful.

Because I use a gelatin-based glue that I cook myself, I leave the panels in the clamps overnight when possible – though I can remove the clamps in an hour if I am in a hurry. Panels made with yellow glue can be released from the clamps in 30 minutes.

For a V-groove, plane both the tongue and the groove boards. For a bead, bead only the tongue board.

AFTER MAKING THE JOINT

If I'm not making a glued-up panel and the boards will be loose, I work the mating edges a bit more. At the least, I use a jack plane to chamfer the long edges that show. This chamfer strengthens the corner to prevent it from splintering off during assembly.

For fancier pieces, I add a small bead to the shoulder of the tongue joint. Don't bead the grooved board unless it is quite thick. The quirk of the bead can weaken the wall of the groove and cause it to splinter off easily.

Lastly, always take into account any seasonal expansion and contraction that will occur with your boards. If making a bunch of unglued backboards or bottom boards, the adage in the Midwest is to work tight in summer (during high humidity time) and loose in winter (low humidity time).

CHAPTER 5

TRENAILS & IRON NAILS

Hungarian-born woodworker Frank Klausz is the most accomplished dovetailer I know. He started cutting the joint as an apprentice in his father's shop to make all sorts of necessary items, from boxes to crates to coffins, for customers.

Why, I wondered, did he cut dovetails for shipping crates? "Why not nails?" I asked him.

"Dovetails were cheaper than nails," he answered.

While none of the projects in this book require dovetails, the point is that wood-to-wood joinery is a less-expensive alternative in communities where iron is scarce or extremely expensive.

The projects in this book can be built without metal fasteners (or even glue). In the place of nails, rived wooden pegs – sometimes called "trenails" or "trunnels" – can be used as the mechanical connection between components.

Trenails can be tapered, like a blacksmith-made nail. There are four sides to the trenail that taper to a rounded point. The trenail is driven into a hole (sometimes tapered, sometimes not), where it gets wedged in place and holds the components together. Then the excess is sawn off. Job done.

Or the trenails can be straight-sided cylindrical pegs that are driven through a mortise and a tenon to hold the joint together. The difference here is that the pilot holes in the mortise and the tenon are offset slightly. So, driving the peg through the holes "draws" the "bores" together. Hence the name, drawboring.

Some people call cylindrical trenails "dowels." That name isn't quite right. Dowels don't have to have dead-straight grain. Trenails do.

A tapered trenail (top) and a cylindrical one.

A hacking knife quickly splits out raw trenails from a board.

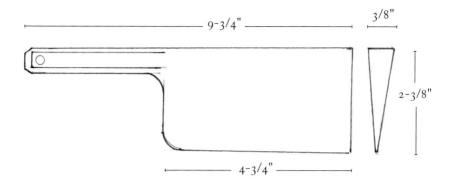

A hacking knife based on Jennie Alexander's tool.

MAKE TRENAILS

Here's how I make trenails. Typically my trenails end up 5/16" square by about 6" long (that's way overlong, by the way). I rive them out of 3/8"-thick dry white oak blanks using a hacking knife. Years ago, I would split off the 3/8" x 3/8" trenails by rapping the back of the hacking knife with a mallet. Now I take the easy route and work on my bench hook. I hold the hacking knife on the blank where I want the split to happen. Then I lift both the hacking knife and oak together, about 4" off the bench. I bring them both down hard. The resulting blow splits the trenail off the blank. Repeat until you have a bunch of rough trenails.

After the trenails are split out, hold one end of the trenail with one hand and shave the tip of the peg to a tapered shape with a 2"-wide chisel. Do this on your bench hook. After I work the tip a bit, I stick it in the shop's pencil sharpener to give it a nice conical shape that is centered on the trenail. Then I taper the four faces of the peg down to the cone. That's about it.

The next step is to drill a 5/16" pilot hole where I want the trenail to go and drive it in with a hammer or mallet. With luck, the trenail will pass through the components and get wedged. And the thicker square section of the trenail will fill the 5/16" pilot hole neatly. Use glue if you like.

To make cylindrical trenails, I start with the same 3/8"-thick blank of wood and split off a bunch of trenails – just like before. But instead of tapering them with a chisel, I drive them through a steel dowel plate, sometimes called a "dowel skinner."

I drive them through the 3/8" hole in the steel dowel plate. Then I sharpen the tip in a pencil sharpener. Finally, I drive them through the 5/16" hole in the dowel plate. Done.

Drive the peg/trenail through the dowel plate to reduce its diameter.

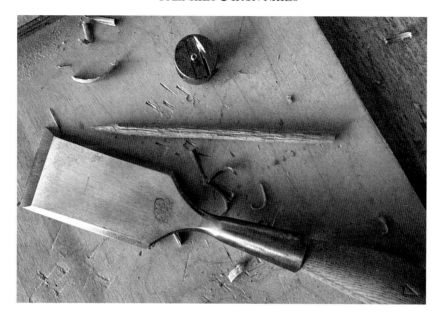

A finished cylindrical trenail.

Typically I use cylindrical trenails for drawboring and tapered ones wherever I would use a metal nail.

METAL NAILS

I like old-fashioned nails quite a bit, and they show up on old work all the time. Wire nails, the modern fastener from the hardware store, will work in a pinch. But I much prefer nails that are square in section and taper along two faces (these are called "cut nails") or taper on all four faces (these are called "Roman nails," "blacksmith nails" or "roseheads").

With cut nails and Roman nails, you need to drill a pilot hole in many instances to avoid splitting the work (in soft woods you can sometimes skip the pilot hole). The pilot hole can be cylindrical or tapered. And it should be half to two-thirds as deep as the length of the nail's shaft.

The diameter of the pilot hole depends on the nail. When using an unfamiliar nail in an unfamiliar species of wood, make some test joints to find the right pilot. The nail should go in with some difficulty, hold like the dickens and not split the work.

There are a lot of kinds of nails with ridiculous names. Skip the names (for now) and simply look at the nail. If it has a prominent flat head, then it is used to hold backboards onto cabinets, case sides to shelves or bottoms onto chests. Anywhere there is difficult fastening work to be done. One common name for

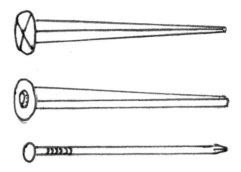

From the top, a Roman nail, a cut nail and a wire nail.

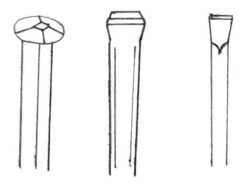

From the left, a rosehead, a brad and a headless brad.

this nail is "rosehead." In the end, the heads of the nails will show prominently, so you have to be OK with that.

If the head is just a slight swelling, most people call these "brads." They are all-purpose nails that can be used in building cabinets (toenailing a shelf in place is a good example) or nailing on heavy trim pieces. Brads can be set below the surface of the wood to make them less visible. But they don't hold as well as roseheads.

The third nail has no real head to speak of. We call these "headless brads" or "pins." They are typically thin and are used to tack veneer or lightweight mouldings in place while the glue dries. This doesn't make them less useful. You just shouldn't expect them to hold the back of a cabinet in place.

Some nails are also made for "clenching." This is when the headed nail

A successful failure. When using a new nail or species, make some test boards to determine the best pilot hole (both depth and diameter).

passes through two pieces of wood and pokes out on the other side. Then the tip is bent and driven back into the wood like a staple. Clenching is commonly used in shipbuilding and when making board-and-batten doors. But it does have its place in furniture as well.

The battens on the doors of the High Carpathian Wall Cabinet are clenched (sometimes written as "clinched"), so the process is discussed in detail there.

This is only a small glimpse into the world of nails.

NAIL LENGTH

The length of the nail is regulated by the ancient "penny system." It's tempting to discard the system until you learn how useful it is. The word "penny" is represented by the letter "*d*." So a 6*d* nail is a six-penny nail.

Example: Let's decide what length of nail you need to fasten some 1/2" backboards to a carcase. First convert the thickness of the board you are nailing down to eighths. So a 1/2"-thick backboard is four/eighths (or 4/8s). The numerator (four) is the penny size you need. You need a 4*d* nail.

[45]

A simple illustration of nail spacing. Put a nail at each end, then center a third nail between them. Divide each remaining space with a nail. Keep going until it's silly.

Let's say you are nailing down 3/4"-thick boards. A 3/4" board converts to 6/8s. Use a 6*d* nail.

Yes, it works with the metric system. Divide the thickness of the board you are fastening down by three and round it as per usual. Nailing down 19mm work? Divide it by three and you get 6.33. Use a 6*d* nail. Like most things in woodworking, you need to use some common sense. If the equation calls for a 7*d* nail and you can't find one for sale, try using a 6*d* nail in hardwoods and an 8*d* nail in softwoods.

If you are unsure, make a test board to try out the combination of nail, pilot hole and boards to see what happens. Adjust.

SPACING NAILS & TRENAILS

One common question among students is: What is the formula or rule-of-thumb for how many nails/trenails to use to fasten a board down?

There isn't one answer. There are a couple ways to do it. My dad taught me to space them one hand-width apart for cabinets (about 4" to 5"). For carpentry, spread out your fingers (about 7" to 8"). That works.

Here's the system I use. Let's say you are fastening a backboard to a cabinet. First drive a nail at the center of the length of the backboard (i.e. for a 36"-

The cut nail on the left has been oriented correctly, and is much less likely to cause a split. The one on the right is oriented incorrectly, and likely will cause a split.

long backboard, drive the first nail at 18"). Then drive nails near the ends of the backboards, usually 2" to 3" from the end of the board.

Now drive nails centered between the center nail and the two end nails. If that doesn't seem to be enough nails, drive nails centered between those nails. Keep going until it's almost ridiculous. I like this system because it always creates a tidy row of nails.

A NOTE ON USING CUT NAILS

Cut nails were dominant in the 19th century and are still made today by a few factories. They are different than Roman nails in that they taper on only two faces. The other two faces are untapered. All the above rules for sizing and spacing and pilot holes apply to cut nails. But there is one small difference.

When you insert cut nails into a pilot hole, orient the nail so the nail's

Nippers come in a variety of sizes. When used with care they will not mar the surface of your work when you pull a nail.

tapered edges cut into the end grain of the board you are fastening down. If you orient the wedge across the grain of the board, you are more likely to split the work. You'll make this mistake once or twice, then the operation will become second nature.

REMOVING NAILS

Pulling nails should be difficult. If it's not, then your pilot hole was too long or too large in diameter. For furniture work, I rarely use the claw on the back end of my hammer. Instead, I use a nipper. I have a small one and a large one. These tools can get under the head of a nail that is nearly flush with the work. And the nipper's jaws are shaped so they are unlikely to mar the work.

Cut nails and Roman nails are far more expensive than wire nails, so I usually keep the bent nails after I pull them. On a rainy day I'll straighten them out on an anvil so they can be used again. Whenever I run out of nails in the middle of a project, I always recall the few bent ones that I thoughtlessly threw away.

CHAPTER 6

GROCERY STORE GLUE

I think you should make your own glue – at least once. It's better than what is on the shelves at the hardware store, it's cheaper and (here's the clincher) you know exactly what is in it.

Last year my shopmate Megan Fitzpatrick and I made about 500 bottles of this glue. We love it and use it on everything from panel glue-ups to tool chests to chairs. It is easy to make using simple ingredients from the grocery.

Now, in the first paragraph of this chapter I said it's "better" than hardware-store glues. Here's what I mean by that.

1. It is as strong as any glue needs to be. What does that mean? When a joint breaks, three things can happen: 1) the glue fails, 2) the wood fails or 3) a little of both happens. In test after test, our test joints suffer only wood failure. And that's all you can ask of a glue.

2. It is reversible. If you mess up, you can plasticize the glue with heat and take the joint apart. You can do this with a wet rag and a clothes iron set to "high" (the water helps transmit the heat to the joint). Or, for deep joinery in thick stock, use a heat gun (used for stripping paint) and wet rags to prevent the wood from scorching. You don't need to scrape the old glue off when reassembling. Simply add more warm glue.

3. It has a sensible open time of about 15-20 minutes, depending on your shop conditions. This glue uses household table salt to slow down the gelling action of the glue. So instead of about 5 minutes of frantic open time (which is what you get with standard yellow glue), you can have a relaxing (well, almost) glue-up.

Here's an industry-standard test of glue. Prepare three identical blocks of wood. Plane their surfaces with care like with any face-grain joint. Glue their faces together with the center one proud. Let the glue cure, then strike the assembly with a hammer. The joint will eventually split due to glue failure, wood failure or a combination of the two.

We measured the gelatin and salt by weight until we felt confident about the consistency of the materials. Then we converted things to volume to speed our production. The recipe in this chapter is mostly by weight.

4. It cleans up easily with hot water – even months or years after it has fully dried.

5. It dries almost completely clear, so you don't get a dark glue line in light-colored woods.

6. It has almost no smell, unless it's been sorely mistreated.

7. It has an indefinite shelf life. Store it in a cool, dry place, and it will last for years.

8. You can easily make its consistency thicker or thinner, depending on your needs. To thin the glue, add a little water. To thicken it, heat it gently so some of the water evaporates. You can do this operation over and over – thick to thin to thick to thin.

The glue is made using three ingredients: food-grade gelatin, noniodized table salt and tap water. You can make a big batch (about 16 ounces) for about $16 – at most. Shopping around can greatly reduce that price.

So why is it important to know what is in your glue? Some people will cite health reasons – like buying organic goods at the grocery. That's not me. I want to know what is in the stuff so I can modify it when necessary and troubleshoot it when something goes wrong.

With Grocery Store Glue, you can easily make it do tricks. Need a longer open time? Add more table salt. Want a fast-tack glue for rub joints? Omit the salt. Need it to be extra flexible because of wood-movement concerns or a special application (like repairing a book)? Add glycerin. There are dozens of published modifications out there for animal-based glue. I am certain that at least some of them work.

ABOUT THE INGREDIENTS

The first ingredient is gelatin, the stuff you get at the grocery to thicken and make jiggly your desserts. Gelatin is perfectly suited to make furniture glue. Gelatin is simply collagen (hide glue) that has been purified to remove the material that gives it a smell and a dark color.

The most common brand of gelatin in the U.S. – Knox – has a bloom strength of 250, which is ideal for furniture joints. "Bloom strength" or "gram strength" is a number given to the gelatin to explain how strong and stiff the stuff is. It's a number from 30 (low strength and jiggly) to 325 (strong, but fragile like glass). A bloom strength of 200 to 250 is a good compromise. That is a strong but flexible wood glue.

You can buy food-grade gelatins at a variety of bloom strengths. If it doesn't state the bloom strength on the package, ask. If they won't tell you, pass on purchasing it.

You'll also see gelatin that is sold in sheets or granules. I prefer the granules, which are more common, as they are easy to measure. You will find some gelatin that is made from cows; others made from pigs. The cow people trash talk the pigs. Don't believe it. Pig gelatin is just as good.

The second ingredient is noniodized table salt. You need fine granules for easy measuring, so pass on the flaky or coarse sea salt. Why skip the iodine? Will it weaken the joint? I don't think so. I've made lots of glue with iodized salt, but I always prefer to make recipes as simple as possible. Noniodized salt is easy to find at the grocery.

The third ingredient is tap water. Feel free to used filtered water if you prefer. We haven't had any problems with water from the tap in the Midwest.

WHAT EQUIPMENT DO YOU NEED?

If you have a kitchen stove, you can make your glue there with a pot filled with water and a thermometer. You can also use a slow cooker, a sous vide immersion heater or any other appliance that can hold temperature at about 140° F (60° C) for a couple hours. We have used wax warmers (for hair removal), coffee-cup heaters and industrial dip tanks. There are lots of options.

You also need a vessel to mix and cook the glue. A clean spaghetti sauce or salsa jar is a good place to begin. After I got fancy, I bought empty HDPE (high-density polyethylene) ketchup squirt bottles at the grocery. When you go this route, you mix the ingredients in the squirt bottle, cook them in the squirt bottle and use it when it's ready to go.

If you own a sous vide immersion heater (a useful cooking appliance), you can easily cook the glue (and reheat it for use). We made hundreds of bottles of glue with this device before switching to industrial equipment.

[55]

HOW TO MAKE THE GLUE

After making 500 bottles, here is the recipe we have settled on. You can add more water (or less) to make a thinner (or thicker) glue. Add another teaspoon of salt to increase the open time.

Grocery Store Glue
- 8 ounces gelatin (by weight). Metric: 226 grams
- 24 ounces (by volume) of hot water. Metric: 710 ml
- 6.5 ounces (by weight) of noniodized salt. Metric: 184 grams

The order of operations is important. Follow the directions with care, and you will end up with beautiful, light-yellow glue with minimal foam at top or junk at the bottom of the bottle. Mix it all nilly-willy, and we'll call it: No Promises Glue.

First get the water running as hot as you can out of your faucet. Add this hot water to the mixing jar. Stir the hot water and add the salt while stirring. Continue to stir until the salt has dissolved. Stir for a minute more.

Now add the gelatin gradually – not all in one dump – while gently stirring the mixture. Don't overdo it – your glue will turn to foam and will be weak.

Here is one of the big advantages of gelatin: You don't have to soak it overnight like you do with hide glue pearls. Fine gelatin granules soak up the water almost instantly.

Heat the mixture in a water bath at 140° to 145° F (60° C) for two hours. Gently agitate the mixture a couple times during the heating process. At the end of the two hours, put the mixture in your refrigerator overnight.

The next day, heat the mixture again at the same temperature for two hours. At the end of the two hours, you might have some white foam at the top of the glue. Remove the foam with a spoon and throw it away. You probably won't be able to remove all the foam but get as much as you can.

You have made liquid hide glue.

You can keep it in the fridge where it will turn to a gel that can be scooped out if you need only a little. It will also be gelatinous at room temperature. To use the glue, first warm it to 140° F (60° C), which is when it will turn runny and easy to brush and pour.

To heat your glue you can use a commercial glue pot or a slow cooker. To heat it, fill the glue pot or slow cooker with water and put the glue bottle in there. It will melt quickly. You can keep it at that temperature for hours without the glue deteriorating. For jobs that are small or quick, you can melt the glue using hot tap water alone (typically 120° to 140° F). Water at that temperature will melt small amounts of glue in short order.

After much testing, we have found no practical limit to the number of times you can heat and cool the glue. I'm sure there is a limit. But if you use a bit of

After the first heat, refrigerate the glue mixture overnight.

the glue each time you heat it (like a normal woodworker), you will never have a problem.

Some things to remember. Consider these friendly hints from your neighborhood pig glue pusher:

1) Don't overheat the glue much past 150° F (65.5° C). That's when it breaks down, loses its adhesive properties and begins to become barbecued jelly.

2) Treat the glue like it's food, because it is food. Very salty food. It's much like beef jerky or fatback, really. But even beef jerky can go bad. Bacteria can attack it (you'll know when this has happened because it will smell rotten

A commercial glue pot is ideal for heating glue for use. The Hold-Heet glue pot (sadly the company is now defunct) holds the temperature at about 125° F.

and/or you'll see black spots on the glue). If you keep the glue's lid closed when you aren't using it and store it in the fridge, you are unlikely to ever have a problem. We have stored some under the bench (out of the sun) and sealed for years. And it's still good.

3) If the glue is too thick in consistency to use after you heat it, add a little water and stir it. If it's too thin, remove the lid and cook the glue for an hour, then stir it again to see if it's to your liking.

Typically we dispense some glue in a paper cup after heating it. Then we apply it to joints with a glue brush. But you can squeeze it right out from the bottle if you prefer.

HOW TO USE THE GLUE

We use a lot of glue in our shop, so we store it in a cabinet where it stays sealed, cool and away from sun. When we start work in the morning with gluing on the agenda, I get out our electric glue pot, fill it with water and heat the glue bottles in that.

While at room temperature, this glue has the texture of a gummy worm (this sentence is foreshadowing). The glue pot heats the stuff to about 125° F, which makes the glue flow nicely. While in the pot, the glue takes about 45 minutes to melt.

What if you don't have a glue pot? You have lots of options. A small slow cooker, wax warmer or even coffee mug warmer will do the trick. Other woodworkers report using baby bottle warmers. Anything that can be turned into a water bath for your glue bottles and can hold that temperature for hours will work.

What about the microwave? I don't recommend it for heating the glue directly. I have used it in a pinch a couple times – short bursts of 5-10 seconds. If the glue (or part of the glue) gets heated up past 150° F, it will lose strength.

However, I am thrilled to use the microwave (or the tea kettle or the stove) to rapidly heat the water that melts the glue, which speeds the process.

When the glue and joinery are ready, here's how it goes.

If I'm gluing housed joints, such as dovetails or mortise-and-tenon joints, I pour some glue into a paper cup and brush it on. If I am assembling an edge joint or a lamination, I squeeze the glue directly out of the bottle.

Then I assemble and clamp as usual, except the process is relaxed because I have 15-20 minutes of open time (thank you, salt).

I clean up the squeeze-out with hot water from the glue pot. Hot water quickens the clean-up. I always leave a little squeeze-out in one obvious place (you'll see why).

Then I walk away. After an hour, I'll check the squeeze-out. If it's soft or rubbery, I leave the clamps on. If it's hard, I take the clamps off.

The glue is sensitive to the temperature in your shop. If you want to speed the drying time, put the assembly in a warm, dry place. Sometimes in cool and damp shops the glue will stay rubbery, even after 12 hours. If it has been 12 hours, go ahead and take the clamps off. It's an animal product and some-times has a mind of its own. (Actually that's a joke. The glue is not intelligent. Instead it is affected by moisture in the wood and the workshop. Waiting 12 hours has always been enough time in the clamps.)

If you are feeling anxiety about using this glue on a piece of your furniture, you are not alone. We have lots of students who experience the same feeling and tell us they were always afraid to use animal-based glues.

But once they used them (usually in class) most converted to using the stuff regularly.

My advice is to try using the glue first on a test joint. Something that has no consequences. It can be as simple as gluing two blocks of wood together.

All glue seems like magic if you think about it much (and I do). You were probably in art class at age 5 when you were told to use a PVA glue (polyvinyl acetate glue – either yellow or white glue). Even then, it took someone else to convince you that this watery substance (about 40 percent water) could form a permanent bond.

So taking that first step by yourself can be difficult. I get it. Now get over it.

AND SOME REALITY

I don't dislike other glues, such as white glue or yellow glue. These are fantastic glues that can be used in challenging environmental conditions. They are strong, backed by science and completely reliable.

You can use them on all the projects in this book and they will last your entire lifetime – easy.

Why use something else?

There are a couple reasons. One is that I like to have control over the entire process, from design to the finish. The glue is an essential element of that process.

Also, animal-based glue is infinitely repairable and reversible. If something goes wrong with my piece some 300 years in the future, a future furniture maker can take the joint apart with heat and moisture, add some more protein-based glue and put the thing back together.

You can't do that with PVA or epoxy.

Animal-based glues are the reason that musical instruments and furniture from 500 years ago is still functional and repairable.

Though this glue costs little to make, its reversibility is almost priceless.

FUN WITH GLUE

OK, this next part isn't totally necessary for this book. But here are a couple things about gelatin-based glue that are amusing and somewhat useful.

1) You can pour it into molds and make funny shapes. There are thousands of cheap silicone molds out there for people who want to make Jell-O shots or weed gummies. You can use these molds to make glue gummies.

Here's how: After the second heat, pour the hot glue into any silicone mold. Put the silicone mold in the fridge so the glue will set up quickly. Then pop the finished glue gummies out of the mold and seal them in a plastic bag. The plastic bag will prevent the glue from drying out and becoming solid gelatin again. (And the bags will repel bacteria.)

We love having these glue gummies around when we need to make a small amount of glue. We pop a couple into a paper cup and stick the cup in our glue pot. In 10 minutes we have just enough glue ready to go for a small job.

2) In a surprise reversal, you can make commercial gummy bears into glue. It's true. Most gummy treats are made of gelatin, water, sugar and some starch. That's not a bad list of ingredients for a glue. Get some gummy worms from the gas station. Put them in a cup and cover them with water. Heat the gummies in a water bath (just like the Grocery Store Glue). In short order you will have a sweet and tasty glue. Add water to thin the glue. Cook it a bit (or add another gummy) to thicken the mixture.

We have used this glue (seriously) on cabinetry. It is reversible – just like hide glue. It is plenty strong. Joints made with gummy glue experience wood

Silicone molds are inexpensive and fun. We made hundreds of glue "gummies" in 2023 as gifts for our friends.

failure – not glue failure – when broken. And your glue line can be an amusing color such as red or green.

This knowledge can be helpful in a pinch. Before we began making our own glue, there were a couple times when I ran out of hide glue before a class. Ordering some was not an option – we needed it that day. So what did I do? I went to the gas station and bought three packs of 99-cent gummy worms. Please don't tell.

CHAPTER 7

FINISHES: HOW TO MAKE & APPLY THEM

When you work in the trades, your personal opinions often come from your boss – the person who trains you and pays you.

My first woodworking job was in a door factory, and I worked mostly in the finishing department. There I developed a respect for glazes and industrial two-part finishes that had to be sprayed while you were in a protective body condom.

Later, at *Popular Woodworking* magazine, we sprayed lacquer in an industrial spray booth on almost everything we made. It was fast, looked good (at first) and made you only a little drunk/sick.

Lacquer was king. My boss at the time had no respect for oils or waxes.

"Those aren't finishes," he said. "They offer zero protection."

I held that opinion for many years until I got old enough to think for myself. And smart enough to stop using finishes laden with toxic volatile organic compounds (VOCs) and heavy metal driers.

These days, I prefer plant-based oils, waxes and paints. Plus other oddball finishes that involve soap, smoke or applying nothing to a piece of furniture.

My sharp turn on finishes began in July 2012 when I visited Peter Follansbee while he was working at Plimoth Plantation (now named the Plimoth Patuxet Museums). Peter took me around the village to see the structures and the furniture inside, most of which he had built during the previous decade or so. I was surprised by how quickly damp dirt floors and smoky fires could make a new piece of furniture look 200 years old. And, most important, the worn pieces were even more beautiful than when they were new.

Both of these pieces at Plimoth are modern, but they aged quickly in the smoky houses with damp dirt floors.

That moment was a turning point. I embraced finishes that looked better with wear: waxes, oils and natural paints. And I began experimenting with oils that were chemically similar to human oil (sebum) and smoke (basically toner powder for a laser printer).

These finishes are not durable – that's the point. They look better the more miles you put on them. And they look best when they are almost totally obliterated by weather, wear and time.

Here are the finishes I now use on pieces that I sell to customers.

BETTER LINSEED OIL

I've become a linseed oil snob and offer no apologies. The "boiled" linseed oil at the hardware store has never been boiled. Instead, poisonous metallic driers have been added to the oil to make it dry faster. The raw linseed oil from the hardware store isn't much better. Instead, I have switched to linseed oils that are refined, purified or blown. These oils can be lighter in weight and color than the hardware store stuff. They dry nicely, penetrate well and yellow the wood a lot less (in my experience).

There are a lot of companies out there making purified/refined linseed oil. It's hard to say which is best. But I can say that every variety of refined oil I have tried is better than the home-center stuff.

Obligatory photo of finishing materials arranged on a workbench. These are some of the purified/refined linseed oils we use in our shop.

I use straight linseed oil when I don't want to add much sheen – just a little protection against water. Mostly I use it on working surfaces: kitchen utensils, cutting boards, workbenches, countertops and the like.

How to apply it: Thin coats are best. Wipe on a fairly wet coat of oil (like when you wipe down your kitchen table). Use a cotton cloth – we prefer surgical towels with a Huck weave. Then use a dry part of the same towel to wipe the surface dry. Wipe until there is no more oil on the surface of the wood. It takes me as long to apply the oil as it does to wipe it off.

Let the oil cure overnight. If the wood looks dry or patchy (it usually doesn't if you did it right the first time) apply a second thin coat.

Lay out your rags flat after you are done finishing. Bunching up rags soaked in linseed oil is a fire hazard. Let them dry before throwing them away or washing them (we wash our Huck towels over and over).

RAW LINSEED OIL & WAX (AKA SOFT WAX)

Most pieces of furniture I make get a coat of soft wax, a linseed oil and wax finish, at some point in the process. This soft wax finish is raw linseed oil, a little beeswax and a tiny bit of citrus solvent (limonene). We cook it in the shop and try to have lots of it on hand.

[65]

Soft wax in the making. The oil is hot. The beeswax has just been added, and I'm pouring in the limonene.

I buy beeswax from Bulk Apothecary, which sells raw ingredients for people who make personal-care products. A pound of beeswax pellets costs anywhere from $5 to $10, depending on how much you order.

You also can get beeswax from beekeepers, which is where I got mine for years. The upside: It's usually inexpensive or free. The downside: You need to refine it to evict the insect parts. (Heat, strain, repeat.)

The second ingredient is raw linseed oil. You can use the hardware store stuff for this recipe, but the refined stuff is better.

People will tell you that raw linseed oil never dries. They are misinformed. Linseed is one of the drying oils. It takes time to fully cure, but if you apply it correctly you can sit in your chair a couple hours after applying this finish.

The third ingredient is just a bit of limonene. This citrus solvent loosens the mixture so it is more of a soft wax (like a heavy peanut butter) and not a bar of soap. You can buy limonene from a variety of sellers and pay anywhere from $1 per ounce to $13 an ounce. I usually pay about $21 for 16 ounces (32 table-spoons). In total, a batch of this finish costs about $7 to $20 to make and will finish more than 10 chairs.

Linseed Oil & Wax Finish Recipe
• 2 cups (16 ounces by volume) raw linseed oil. Metric: 473 ml
• 3.8 ounces (by weight) shredded beeswax. Metric: 108 g
• 2-4 tablespoons limonene. Metric: 30-60 ml

I make this finish in a metal quart paint can from the hardware store. Place the metal can on a hotplate, fill the can with the raw linseed oil and turn on the hotplate to between low and medium. Monitor the temperature with a cooking thermometer. Beeswax melts at 151° F (66° C). As soon as the temperature of the oil reaches 151°, pour the beeswax pellets and limonene into the oil. The amount of limonene determines how stiff the finish will be. Use 2 tablespoons of limonene for a finish that is like hard ice cream – you'll need a spoon to dish it out. Use 4 tablespoons for something you can scoop out with your fingers.

Stir the mixture with a stick until the beeswax melts (it should take about a minute). Turn off the hotplate and remove the mixture from heat.

Allow it to cool. It will become a paste after about an hour of cooling. Seal. You can use it immediately or keep it indefinitely.

How to apply: I wipe on the soft wax with a 3M non-woven gray pad (available at hardware stores). The pad is a tad abrasive, so it knocks down any fuzzy bits of wood you missed. With wax finishes, the important question is this: When do I start wiping/buffing?

Too soon and you take most of the wax off. Too late and the wax becomes difficult to buff.

Luckily, this finish is mostly oil, so you have a big window of time. I usually apply the soft wax to about half of a chair then buff. Then I apply it to the other half of the chair and buff. Then I buff the whole thing to make sure I didn't miss any spots.

We use surgical towels (Huck towels) to buff off the soft wax. The towels have a little texture and are quite absorbent – they are perfect for this finish. Then leave the finish alone for about two hours. After that, you can use the object. It will take a couple weeks for the oil to fully cure.

Again, lay out your rags flat after you are done finishing. Let them dry so you don't create a fire hazard. Wash them to reuse them.

Soft wax can go on bare wood, or over most painted surfaces (it looks great over milk paint). The key to success is to use thin coats.

Megan and I have been using linseed oil paint a lot during the last two years. It has a learning curve, but it is worth the effort.

If you are asking yourself: But will this go over <insert finish type here>? Then definitely do a test board first.

LINSEED OIL PAINT

Years ago I experimented with linseed oil paint, and I am now a convert. The upside: If you do it right, the paint covers in one coat. The downside: It can take a few days to a week to dry.

In its simplest form, linseed oil paint is pigment plus linseed oil. Some manufacturers add driers to make the paint dry faster. Some manufacturers use refined linseed oil. How you thin it and apply it has a lot to do with the final result. It's not difficult to use. It just takes a little practice to get used to its properties – just like learning to use hide glue or shellac.

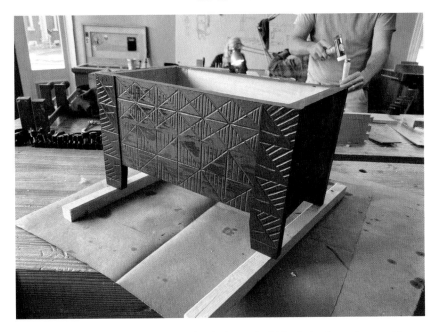

Linseed oil paint can take up to a week to dry. And it can look blotchy in places when wet. Be patient.

Before you paint, many experts recommend you apply a coat of raw/purified linseed oil to the bare wood. This seems to make the paint go on easier.

Also, before painting, make sure the paint is fully mixed. Linseed oil paint is difficult to mix if the solids have settled. The best way to mix it up is to make friends with the employees at your local hardware store. They can usually shake the paint with their paint-shaking machines. This will save you almost an hour of tedium.

BRUSHES

Linseed oil paint can be brushed on with synthetic or natural bristles. The brush produces the final surface texture (linseed paints do not self-level), so you want a brush that is dense with fairly stiff bristles. It is also helpful to have a second, dry brush to "tip off" the final surface (that is, a light brush stroke that further draws out any furrows, to eradicate them).

The brushes are more difficult to clean than when using water-based paints. One strategy is to use linseed oil soap to clean the brush. A second strategy is to simply suspend the brush in linseed oil and designate a brush for each color of paint you use. A third strategy: Pitch the brush when you are done.

When dry, linseed oil paint allows the pores and texture of the wood to shine through.

THINNING & THIN COATS

You can thin linseed oil paint with more linseed oil (which reduces the amount of pigment) or with turpentine (which makes the paint less viscous). A little turpentine makes the paint flow more easily. There are many recipes out there for thinning the paint quite dramatically for an initial coat, then using full-strength coats at the end. This, of course, means you have to apply more than one coat.

Our recommendation is to shoot for one-coat coverage. Thin the paint if you need to, or work with it right from the jar. The goal is to stretch the paint as thin as you can – much, much thinner than with latex or acrylic. And to work the paint with the brush to get as smooth a finish as possible. After painting a section, tip off the paint with light strokes using the tips of a dry brush. Then move on. Try not to rework sections of the finish unless you have to.

The paint dries slowly, so take your time. Draw out the film as much as you can before recoating the brush. When you think you can't draw it out any more, try. Put your brush back where you started, then draw it out farther. When you truly can't draw it out more, use the dry brush to tip off, then move on.

DRYING

Temperature and sunlight seem to encourage linseed oil paint to dry. Let the paint dry for a couple days before even touching it. And then touch it only on an unseen surface. If it feels soft and rubbery, leave it alone. When it feels dry and a little scratchy, let it sit for a couple more days. Note that it may dry with a different sheen in some areas than in others. The next step usually takes care of that – and if it doesn't, time will.

After the linseed oil paint is completely dry, we usually add a thin coat of soft wax or refined linseed oil to the surface with a 3M gray pad. This smooths the surface and adds a little sheen. Let the oil and/or wax dry overnight before using the item.

While the drying time of the paint seems a fault, I actually don't mind it. I set the piece aside for a while and work on other pieces.

When the paint is finally done, it has a tactile quality you don't get with latex or acrylics. And the more you use the piece, the better it looks. Because the paint isn't a hard film, it wears differently. It doesn't crack. It ages more like the erosion of a stream bed, gently revealing the wood beneath.

THE FINAL FRONTIER

I have experimented with finishes for most of my adult life. And this book isn't the end of that process. As I type these words I've been mixing carbon black with jojoba oil to imitate years of skin contact and exposure to smoke.

Most of all, don't discount time as your partner when finishing. Wood and oils and wax and ultraviolet light conspire to mellow the pieces we make. Most of the items I make look quite brash to my eye when they are freshly finished. I've come to expect and rely on the fact that time and the environment will finish the job that I simply started.

CHAPTER 8

A WALK AROUND THE SYMBOLIC BLOCK

"God is the name of the blanket we throw over mystery to give it shape."
— *Barry Taylor, AC/DC's road manager.*

Our world is awash in symbols and signs. Some of them we are aware of. But most of them pass through us like rented corn.

After studying the symbols common to Scandinavia, the Baltics and Eastern Europe, I began to see echoes of them everywhere. One day I was walking to our shop after lunch, and was stopped cold by the cast iron storm drain on West 7th Street. I have stepped over this thing 1,000 times without a second glance.

But this time I saw it: the "fishing net" spell.

It's a protection spell (in some cultures) consisting of diagonal lines that create a net of rhombus shapes. A bit like chain-link fence. The spell is supposed to "catch" evil, disease or other unfortunate events.

Of course, the incised diamond pattern on the drain has a practical purpose. It is supposed to catch rainwater and prevent it from pooling on top of the storm drain. This makes it safer for pedestrians. But the incised pattern could have been almost any pattern – it didn't have to be the fishing net to serve its purpose.

This is the curious part for me. I do not think these geometric patterns were placed intentionally. But they came from somewhere. Just like most (if not all) Americans came from somewhere else during the last 30,000-plus years.

My neighborhood was settled by Germans in the late 19th century. The houses are mostly full masonry construction (as opposed to wooden frame construction), which is unusual for the U.S. And almost every home in our neighborhood is covered in some kind of geometric ornament. Usually it's on the lintels over the windows and doors. But it can extend to almost any part of the structures.

Let me repeat something before you give me shit about it: I don't think the 19th-century builders meant to transmit a message with these symbols. These are merely pleasing geometric shapes that were likely familiar to the European immigrants. The symbols' meanings were likely already lost by the 1890s when these buildings were constructed by German masons. But the marks were compelling enough to make the long journey through the centuries in Europe, the long boat ride across the Atlantic and on to the façades of many homes and businesses.

They are here for us now to consider anew.

The following photos were taken during an 8-minute walk around the block in my neighborhood. Up Willard Street and around West 8th Street. Down Greer Street. And back down West 9th Street to our building. I photographed ornaments on only a handful of the houses. The structures on our block are literally awash in geometric symbols. Here's what I saw.

A PERSON, A SOUL

One of the most common symbols I've seen on old Eastern European furniture (and the buildings in my neighborhood) is one that represents a person. The symbol is usually a circle that has an "X" through it. The X can also be thought of as a Christian cross, or a slanted cross. But the oldest meaning (as far as I can tell) is that this is the symbol for a person or a soul.

Sometimes this X is inside of a circle, and sometimes it stands alone.

BOUNTY OR PLENTY

Another common symbol in Eastern European furniture is overlapping arcs, which can represent plowed fields. These symbols are everywhere in my neighborhood as well. At first, I called this typical Victorian ornament "fish scales." But after seeing it in so many different configurations engraved on Eastern European furniture, I began to think of it as something else. As a representation of plowed fields and bountiful food (which makes more sense than fish scales on a house in the landlocked Middle West).

ROSES & OTHER FLOWERS

There are many rose patterns on old furniture and on buildings. They can have four, six or eight petals. Roses carry many meanings in the Western world. One meaning we all agree on is beauty.

Typical "person" symbols: A circle with an X through it.

Fish scales? Or plowed fields?

A four-petal rose on the building across the street from us (above). More four-petal roses (below).

Lots to see above. Teeth. The fishing net. And diamonds….

The three symbols at the top of this lintel could be sun symbols.

AND THE ONES I WONDER ABOUT

Once you open your eyes to these symbols, you might encounter ones you cannot explain. They could be purely decorative, of course, but I've found that a little more study and pondering will turn up some possible meanings.

Then there are the bright diamonds found on the lintel above. I haven't (yet) seen these on old furniture. But they interest me. Also, note the fishing net spell between the two diamonds. And the teeth (more on the teeth soon).

Everything shown above might be completely devoid of meaning. They are just slashes found on hundreds of houses in our city. Or the slashes are trying to communicate something. The masons who "wrote" them down in the 19th century might not have known how to spell or conjugate.

But the message is still there. And maybe we can learn the language, take something from it for ourselves and pass it on.

[79]

Spell panel No. 106. It might seem corny to engrave an image of your family, but I recommend it.

THE SPELL IS COMPLETE

After studying the symbols, I wanted to make them. Because the engraving tools used by Eastern European artisans were unknown in these parts, I needed to make my own or find tools from another trade that might do the job.

I spent months grinding and shaping tools from scratch. When those didn't work to my satisfaction, I hired blacksmiths to make some tools, and I modified those. I also tried some leatherworking tools that looked kinda like the old engraving tools. And when I struggled with those tools, I considered (briefly) plugging in my router.

Lucky for me, I've been this dumb before.

When I first learned to sharpen edge tools, I tried every method ever mentioned. I bought jigs, stones, magic clay and special leather. Nothing worked. But after struggling for months, the waters parted and suddenly all the stones, systems, jigs and fairy dust worked.

My problem with sharpening wasn't the jigs or the stones. It was me. I hadn't practiced enough to get a good edge every time.

I realized I needed to spend some serious time at the bench with the engraving tools.

I didn't want to practice engraving on scrap wood because the stakes were too low. So, I resolved to make 100 or so "spell panels." Each panel was a 3/4" x 6" x 6" piece of basswood. Thanks to their size and shape I could easily grip them in my face vise and engrave them. Because of their small size, I could easily engrave seven or eight panels a day during a break from another job. And because I had 100 of them to do, I had lots of opportunities to try different tools.

By the time I got to my 100th panel, I could see a marked improvement in my work. And I could switch with ease between the blacksmith-made tools, the leather tools and any other round-cutting gizmo that was handy.

I started by engraving simple patterns: lines and arcs. Then I combined the two to make some simple spells. By the end, I tried to cram as many different spells onto a panel as possible without it looking like an old wooden middle school desk.

Then I ventured into engraving human forms, such as a praying farmer or a portrait of a woman of great resolve.

With practice, the human figures I engraved were livelier. My engraved lineweights varied more and more with each spell, which added dimension to each composition. And everything looked more fluid after engraving thousands of curved and straight geometrical forms.

This was the result I had hoped for. But something else happened that I hadn't planned on.

The month I spent engraving spell panels marked 10 months since my cancer surgery, and my recovery had been just as the doctor said it would be, which

Some of the 100-plus spell panels I engraved as I learned to master the engraving tools.

is to say, agonizingly slow. The biggest struggle wasn't that I peed my pants all day. In fact, I'd come to employ it (almost enjoy it) as a weapon. When someone said something mean to me, I'd secretly pee my pants at them.

Instead, the biggest challenge was my physical endurance. Early on after the surgery I found I was working too hard, and I almost ended up back in the hospital. So I dialed down my to-do list for each day. And I pushed work off onto my co-workers.

On good days, I was operating at about 70 percent of where I was before the da Vinci robot had its way with my innards.

But during the last two weeks of carving spells, there was a change.

All of the "spells" – or wishes or prayers or whatever – that I engraved were positive and life-affirming ideas. Most of the spells involved some sort of protection from bad things. Protection for your family. The land. The earth. Your food. Unborn children.

Other spells were wishes for eternal love. Or a reminder to live every day to its fullest because we have only so much time left on the earth.

Now I don't put much stock in a higher power. But at some point during the spell casting I became convinced that my body was back at 100 percent. Perhaps this just happens 10 months after surgery, or maybe it was some self-delusion caused by immersing myself in the ancient equivalent of being trapped inside a Hallmark store.

One Thursday morning, I woke up and decided to attempt a full-on day of everything physical and mental I could muster. It was easy and exhilarating. I tried again on Friday and Saturday, pushing myself as hard as when I was in my 20s.

I carved one more panel, my 106th. It was a spell I had never tried before. Four people standing on the earth, which was wrapped with a protection spell called the fishing net. This is us: Me, Lucy, Madeline and Katherine. Protected.

I thought I was going to cry a little. But then I hiccuped and peed my pants instead.

I wonder if there's a spell called "the clothespin."

CHAPTER 9

SOME COMMON SYMBOLS & SPELLS IN EUROPE

Symbols consisting of straight lines and arcs have been a part of human culture for thousands of years. Attempting to catalog and understand them is something that archaeologists and ethnologists have been doing for almost as long as people have been creating them.

Aleksandra Dzērvītis, a chronicler of geometric symbols, says that human cultures first started using geometric symbols in connection with religion in the Neolithic Era (ca. 7,000–1,700 B.C.E.). These symbols were later adopted and adapted by the Christian religion as that faith spread across Europe.

For this book, I focus on symbols that appear on decorative objects (furniture, clothing and other household goods) in European peasant cultures.

When I use these symbols in my work, I do not mix and match symbols from one region, such as Scandinavia, with those from other cultures, such as the United Kingdom, Italy or Eastern Europe. While there are remarkable similarities in the shape of the symbols used among these different cultures, I don't want to engrave a chest with symbols of a growing family that could be interpreted as something more like a 1997 GMC Amber Alert van (with no windows).

You do have to be careful with your lines and arcs.

Gyenes Tamás puts it this way in his book "Ácsolt ládák titkai" (any errors in translation are my fault):

We can roughly decipher visual signs, but no one should expect us to say to a sign: THIS or THAT is the exact meaning. It is difficult to determine the meaning of a circular sign, a tulip, by itself, because it is so widespread in Hungarian folk art. But its interpretation is complete when viewed in the whole composition, and it is possible to talk about it more precisely there. At the same time, this is what makes our Hungarian folk art exciting, because it requires imagination and the ability to vary – both in the creation and in the reading – because if the symbols were too rationally and rigidly defined, then only mechanical, boring pattern sets would emerge from them (as they have also developed elsewhere).

The following sections are separated along political or ethnic lines. This is not an attempt to divide cultures, but merely to point out what symbols appear in each country. How you use them is up to you.

UKRAINE

These symbols and their meanings are taken from "Ukrainian Design Book: Book 1" by Natalie Perchyshyn *et al* (Ukrainian Gift Shop, Minneapolis, Minnesota).

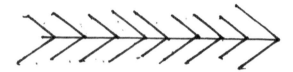

Pine needles: Long life, youth, virility and health. Many European cultures use evergreen trees to signify long or everlasting life.

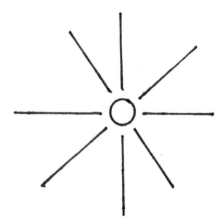

Flowers: Life, growth, love, charity. Many other cultures also draw the flower simply to represent beauty.

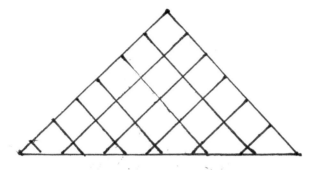

The fisher's net: While in many cultures this symbol is a protection spell (the net catches evil things), the Ukrainian symbol today relates to Christian proselytizing. Jesus told his apostles to be "fishers of men."

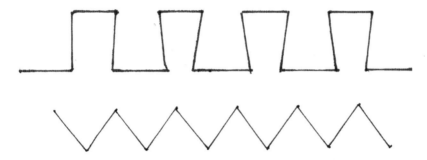

The meander: Eternity. The unbroken and moving line is often used to represent eternity or the repetitive or circular nature of life. Sometimes the meander line can look like "wolf teeth," a protection spell in other cultures.

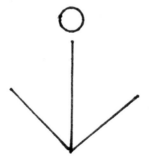

Plant symbols: New life, happiness, growth and a good harvest. Many cultures use plant symbols in similar ways. The plant symbols may look different from culture to culture, but their meanings are similar.

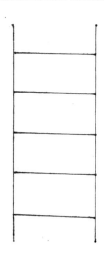

Ladder: Prayers, ascending to heaven.

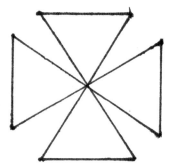

Cross: There are dozens of variations on this symbol, which represents Christ and his suffering on behalf of others. In pre-Christian cultures, the cross could mean a person or soul.

Saw: A triangular symbol (sometimes also used as a meander) indicating fire, or heat that sustains life.

Wolf teeth: Loyalty, wisdom and a firm grip. As you will see, these triangular lines can be interpreted different ways.

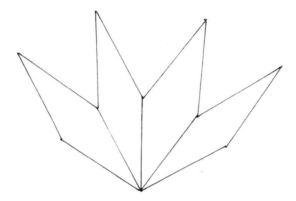

Half stars: Purity and light.

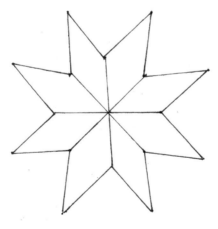

Full star: The eye of God or the love of God for people.

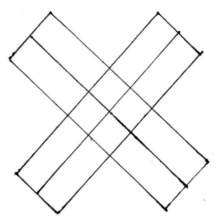

St. Andrew's cross: The X-shaped cross that St. Andrew was crucified on.

LATVIA

These symbols are from "Latvian Design" by Aleksandra Dzērvītis (1972, 1976, Parr's Print & Litho Limited, Toronto).

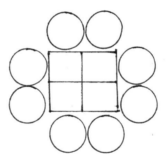

The sun: This symbol can be as simple as a circle or as complex as you like. It represents light and life.

The moon: A rare symbol to find on furniture as it is used to represent death. It is typically found on the bracelets of warriors.

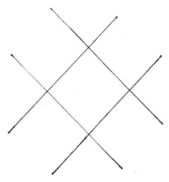

The cross-hatch star: A common and long-used symbol that protects people during the night.

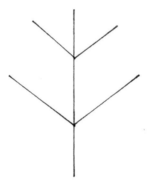

Austra's tree: The tree of the sun, with golden branches, copper roots and silver leaves.

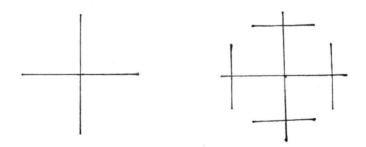

Cross and the cross of crosses: In a pre-Christian context, these symbols represented stars in Latvian songs and poetry. The cross of crosses was sometimes used on sacrificial stones.

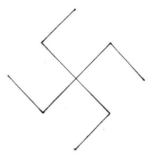

The thunder or fire cross: In ancient cultures, this symbol represented fire, life, light, health, prosperity. Because of its adoption by the Nazis of the 20th century, it is rarely used today.

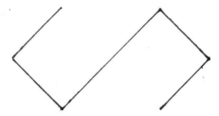

The serpent: A symbol used since the Iron Age to designate well-being.

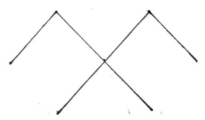

Jumis: A two-eared stalk of grain that represents fertility and prosperity.

Mara: The zig-zag in Latvian culture is the protector of the farmer's cattle, and water and the life in the water.

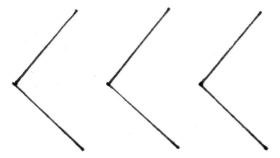

Laima: The goddess of destiny. It is supposed to look like a broom (which was used to help save drowning people) or the twig of a fir tree. In Latvian culture the fir twig is associated with death, and it can symbolize the soul.,

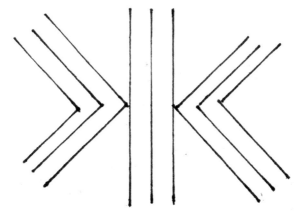

Laima's broom: Laima resides under the threshold of a house, so nothing should ever be handed over the threshold lest it disturb Laima. This broom symbol is a common protection glyph. Even in Colonial New England you will find old houses where a broom has been installed under the threshold of a house to protect it.

THE UNITED KINGDOM

Most of these symbols have been written about by Timothy Easton, M.J. Champion, C.J. Binding and L.J. Wilson in papers for the academic and popular press.

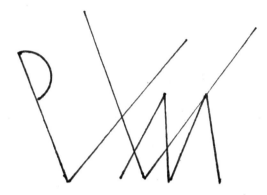

W, P, R and M: A scribed or engraved W is likely to represent the Virgo Virginum (the virgin of virgins) – Mary, the mother of Christ. When a P appears it is often near an R or X and you have the Chi-Rho symbol, a Christogram or the representation of Jesus. Some scholars see the P alone as associated with Puella (a girl), which may or may not be a female saint. When the P is close to the M and W, it could be a plea to the virgin to bring peace to the house.

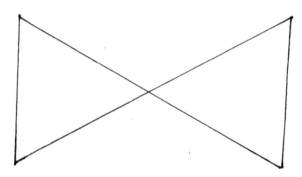

Butterfly cross: An evil-averting symbol. But it can also be a carpenter's symbol for plumb and level.

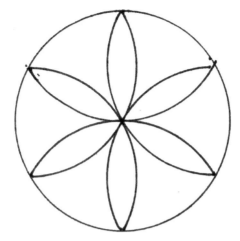

Hexafoil: The daisy wheel can be traced back to the 6th century B.C.E. as a symbol for the sun. It can be interpreted generally as a good-luck symbol. And it averts the evil eye.

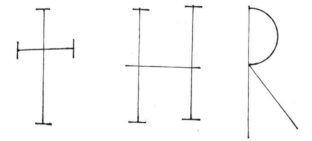

The crossed I: Represents the first letter of Jesus' name.

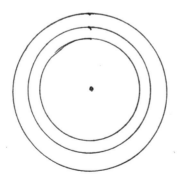

Witch mark: Concentric circles inside one another were engraved in (or near) hearths to prevent witches from entering the structure when they were in the form of animals. The witch was supposed to see the mark and become trapped in the endless circles.

ROMANIA

These symbols are taken from a paper on pristolnic (a holy bread seal) by Ana-maria Stanescu, "Pristolnic: Orthodox object of worship in the traditional household."

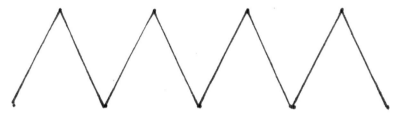

Wolf teeth: The symbol of a guardian or protector.

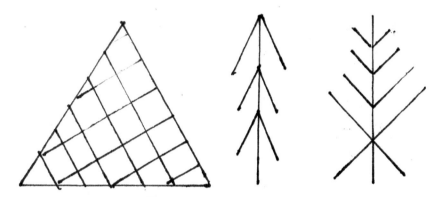

Mountain and the tree: Frequently used together, the tree is a symbol of eternal life.

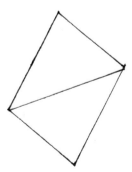

Rhombus: Two triangles attached at their base. This symbolizes masculine and feminine, heaven and earth, or harmony. It can be a symbol of love or fertility.

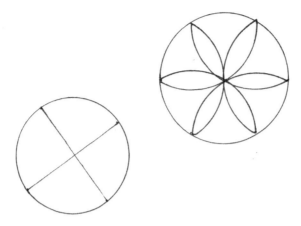

Sun: These two symbols were used by the cult of the sun and represent light spreading to humanity.

HUNGARY

The following symbols and their meanings are taken from Tamás' "Ácsolt ládák titkai."

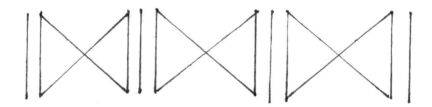

Square or slanted cross: The germ of life, a soul.

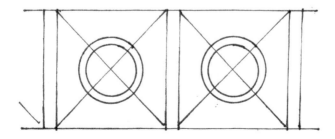

Crosses with circles: A person embodied in the real world. A specific person.

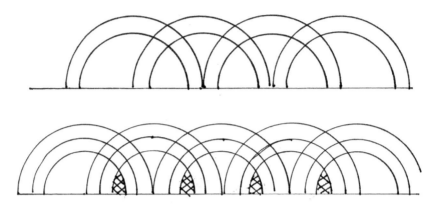

Arched row: Life on earth. Plowed land. Sometimes with seeds sown in between the rows. It can, in certain contexts, be used to express the life-giving wheat field, children being born or the parable of Jesus.

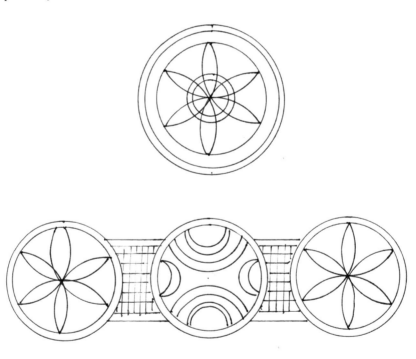

Circular signs: These are usually displayed as three symbols with one in the middle being different. This can represent a marriage, with God between them. If there are connecting lines among these symbols, those can indicate love, which binds them.

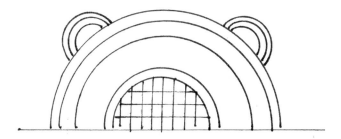

Semi-circle signs: Similar to the interconnected arcs, these are usually found on the bottom boards of chests. They remind us of the setting sun, of burial mounds, of the final slumber. The additional semi-circles represent "pearls" of dignity, respect and wisdom gained during life.

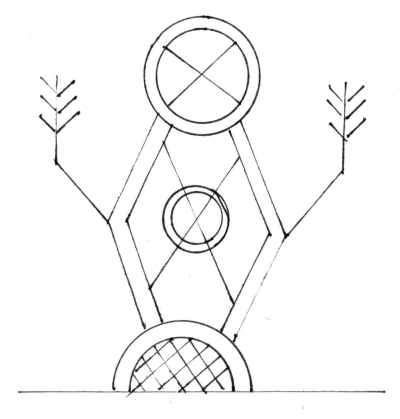

Images of people: These are depicted on semi-circles representing the earth. (I think it looks like their hands might be held up in prayer.) They appear to be looking up, and the lid of the chest represents the heavens.

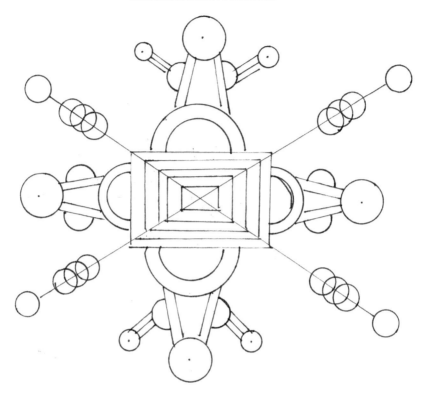

A family around a table.

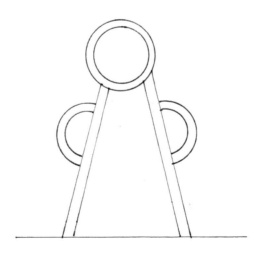

A human or an angel; perhaps standing in silence.

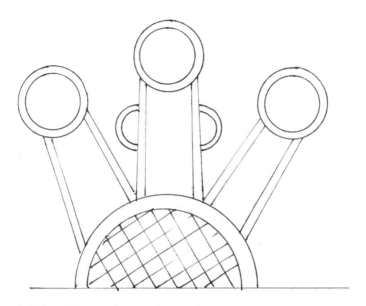

A family on a hill: The middle one is drawn as the active figure.

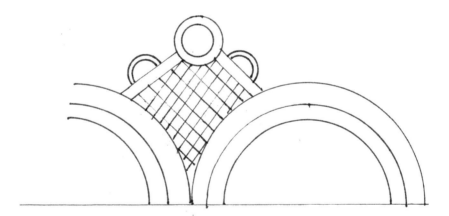

A person with two setting suns behind them.

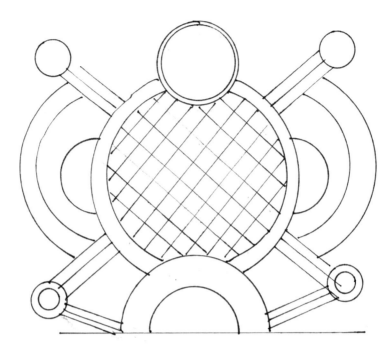

An angel ascending.

SYMBOLS TODAY

As I first began to study these symbols, I wasn't entirely clear what their meanings were. So I'd stare at them until my eyes became blurry and I entered into a bit of a trance-like state. Then some of the shapes became obvious, especially the symbols for the sun and plowed fields.

But other times my brain traveled to other places. Images of grids started to look like the cells of a spreadsheet or the drop ceiling in some class-A office space, complete with some rectangles that were filled in with lines (the fluorescent lighting).

Concentric circles became the Wi-Fi symbol. And the slanted cross looked like an hourglass or the symbol for eternity (or both).

I think I'm trying to say that the geometry of straight lines and arcs could be used to create a pattern language that reflects the joys and anxieties of the current day.

These geometrical constructions can also be used to create almost any animal you can think of. Artist Charley Harper (1922-2007) used straight lines and arcs to generate many of his playful beasts and bugs. If you love animals, I encourage you to investigate his work and use it as a springboard to create your own pattern language.

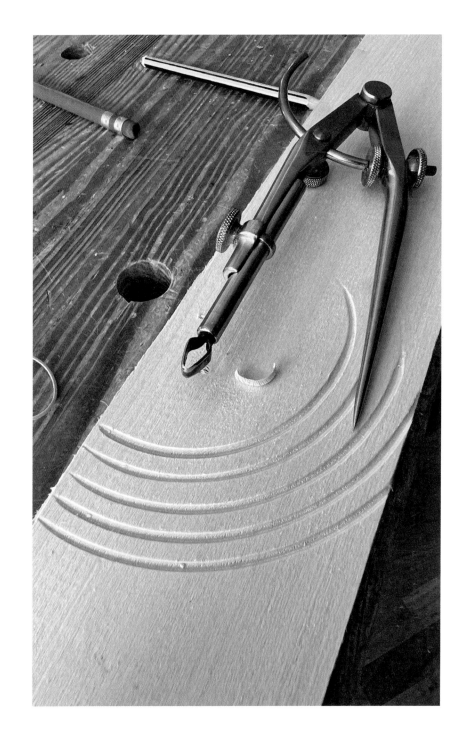

CHAPTER 10

SHARPEN & USE ENGRAVING TOOLS

Many of my favorite peasant pieces are engraved with straight lines and arcs. These engravings are decorative, symbolic or (if you have an open mind) magical or religious in nature. From a distance, the engravings look like they might have been scratched in, perhaps with a compass, awl or V-tool. But close inspection reveals the truth: The engravings are shallow, U-shaped channels that travel across the grain, at an angle to the grain and parallel to the grain – all in continuous lines.

The traditional tools that engrave these lines are not common in the West. The traditional cutter is shaped a bit like a fishing hook and is mounted in a knife-like handle to make straight cuts or in a compass to make arcs.

After studying videos, photos and drawings of the old tools, I realized that the cutter resembled the business end of a race knife or a timber scribe. These two tools are common in Western woodworking, so that's where I began my search for an inexpensive engraving tool.

The race knife and timber scribe were used in workshops, on job sites and by those who cut timber to mark their possessions or keep track of the pieces in a complex assembly.

For example, after cutting down a tree, a sawyer might engrave the butt of the tree with a personal mark indicating that they should get credit for the tree when it arrived at the sawmill. The race knife has an integral awl that allows you to scribe arcs of a single radius, plus straight lines. In other words, you can engrave the entire alphabet with a race knife.

A timber framer might use a timber scribe, which makes only straight lines,

The two tools in the middle are vintage race knives. They each have two cutters: one for making straight-line cuts and a second for making arcs of a fixed radius.

A timber scribe has only one cutter. You can use it against a straightedge for straight cuts, or against a curved template for curves.

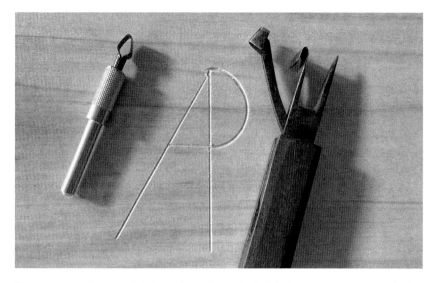

You can engrave the entire alphabet with a timber scribe (right). Or use an engraving tool (left), with the addition of a straightedge and compass.

to mark the components of a joint with Roman numerals. These numbers help ensure that IX tenon goes into IX mortise. And in a workshop, you sometimes see the mark of a timber scribe on the back of old drawers, indicating this was the III drawer that fits into the III space in a cabinet carcase.

But it's rare to see marks from these tools used as ornamentation. In Western work, woodworkers instead used carving tools to create low-relief decoration on woodwork – not engraving tools.

I bought a couple antique race knives and a handful of timber scribes to attempt some simple engravings – plus to get a feel for sharpening cutters with this fishhook shape. After getting the hang of these tools, I paid two blacksmiths to make tools that resembled the ones from Eastern Europe.

The blacksmith-made tools worked well after some tuning, but because they are handmade, they are rightfully expensive. I didn't want my chapter on engraving tools to begin with the sentence: First pay a blacksmith $100 to $1,000 to make you some engraving tools.

So, I looked around to find a simple tool – perhaps something that was already mass-manufactured for some other industry – that could be adapted to engrave these decorative spells.

I filled a large metal toolbox with all the near misses: leather-cutting tools, hoof knives, girdling tools and dozens of tools used in ceramics. None were suitable (or adaptable) for engraving both straight lines and arcs in wood.

Then reader Bert Bleckwenn sent me a photo of a pear-shaped cutter that

Some of the early engraving cutters that blacksmith Peter Ross made for me.

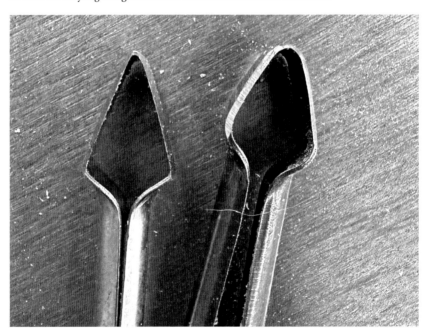

The pear-shaped vinyl cutter on the right is ideal. The one on the left is difficult to sharpen. Both are available world wide (with some effort).

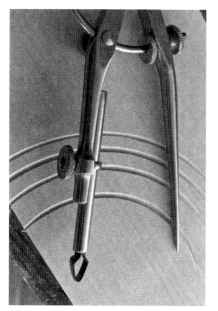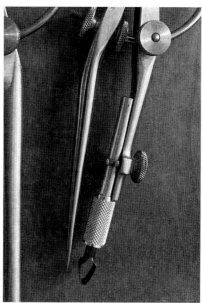

I am forever grateful to Bert for finding these vinyl flooring cutters. The way he came up with to hold the cutter is simpler in many ways (left). But we wanted the blades to be easily interchangeable. So we used a collet to hold the cutters (right).

was used to shave the welds when installing vinyl flooring. Stamped and bent from thin steel, the cutters looked about the right size and shape. But was the steel any good? And what was the best way to grasp the cutters in both a knife handle and in a compass? (The typical knife handle used in the vinyl flooring trade wasn't the answer.)

Bert had made a simple tool holder by drilling a small hole in the end of a short steel rod that was about the diameter of a round pencil. The cutter fit into the rod with friction or epoxy. Then the rod slid into a compass.

His tool worked great. The cutters turned out to be easy to sharpen, and they held an edge quite well, considering how cheap they were. While I used pear-shaped cutters at first, I found there was far too much variation in the way they were manufactured. Some pear-shaped cutters had a point that was nicely rounded. Some were too pointed.

So, I switched to using round cutters. They are consistent and work quite well. (Though I still like the pear-shaped cutters that aren't too pointy.)

For the tool's handle, I wanted something that allowed the cutters to be swapped out easily. I found an aluminum knife used in the crafting world that could hold the cutters. I turned the knife handle down on my lathe so it could be installed in a compass to engrave arcs. And it also could be used like a pen-

The round cutters are more consistent (as far as their manufacturing goes) and easier to sharpen. The line they make is a little wider than with the pear-shaped cutters, but is likely better overall.

cil to cut straight lines (with the guidance of a wooden straightedge).

I made several prototype tools on my wood lathe to find the best diameter and length. You can, too. The craft knife I started with is the Excel K2 (about $6 in 2024). You can find it in hobby stores all over the world.

To turn down the handle, I clamped it in my lathe's Nova chuck, which is used for small face plate work. I turned down a section of the handle so it would fit into my pencil compass (typically this is a little less than .30" – but check your compass first).

I used a straight carbide cutter typically used for roughing out wooden blanks. You also can use a cutter with a slight radius. After every few seconds of cutting, I'd add some lubricant. Don't get aggressive with your carbide tool. Think of aluminum as just a fairly hard wood, and you'll do fine.

After turning down the pencil-sized section, remove the waste. You can part off the waste. Or use a hacksaw.

If you don't want to turn aluminum, you can buy a tool from us at Crucible Tool that is ready to go and includes two of the cutters. Total cost to the consumer: $27 (this was in 2024). Here endeth the advertising.

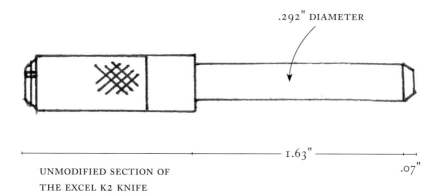

.292" DIAMETER

1.63"

.07"

UNMODIFIED SECTION OF
THE EXCEL K2 KNIFE

We make our engraving tool handles from an Excel K2 knife handle. We turn down one end of the knife so it fits into a typical pencil holder in a compass. The collet section shown on the left is unmodified.

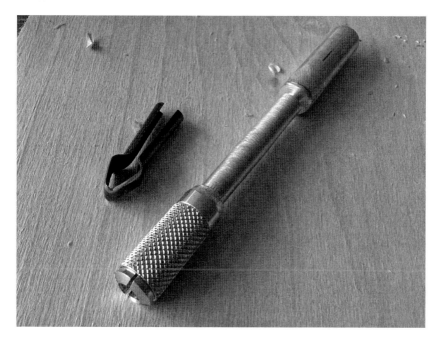

Turning aluminum is simple work (with a little lubricant). After reducing the diameter of the handle so it would fit into the compass, I removed the handle from the lathe's chuck and sawed off the thick part of the handle.

[111]

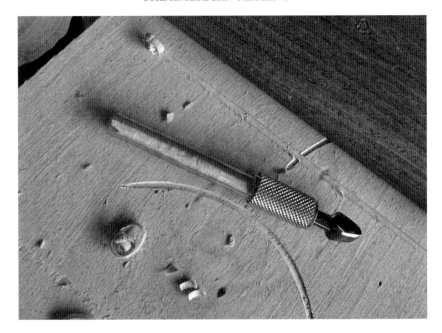

The pear-shaped cutter in the knife handle.

Note to people in the far-flung future (assuming there is one): The cutters should be available as long as vinyl flooring still exists. Find some of these cutters and make a handle from steel or aluminum that is pencil-shaped and less than .30" in diameter. Then cast spells to save yourself.

SHARPEN THE ENGRAVING CUTTER

No matter where you bought your engraving cutter or its shape, you can sharpen it using common tools and simple methods. It's best to have a cutter that is thin in cross section, with very little bevel on the outside of the tool.

A shallow bevel on the outside of the cutter makes it easier for you to start the engraving cut.

Because the cutter needs to cut in both directions for best results, you need to sharpen both sides of the cutter. If you are using a vinyl flooring blade, one side of the cutter should have a rough bevel from the factory. The other side will be blunted and dull.

The cutter's steel is thin, so it is easy to sharpen. Here's how to begin.

Install the cutter in the aluminum handle to make it easy to move as you work. Shape both cutting edges with a smooth-cut file or a flat needle file. I prefer a Nicholson 6" half-round double-cut smooth file for this operation. Brace the tool's handle against the edge of a workbench while filing. The

[112]

Sharpening is simple. File the bevels on the cutter to remove any bluntness. Polish the bevels with fine automotive sandpaper affixed to a piece of wood. Then polish the interior of the cutter with a fine cylindrical oilstone. The procedure is exactly the same for the round cutters.

These inexpensive cylindrical oilstones are useful for many tools besides the engraving cutter.

engraving tools cut only about 1/16" deep, so don't work the tool's entire edge – just the curved shape at the tip of the cutter.

Make the bevels on either side of the tool as identical and as shallow as possible with the file. It shouldn't take much work.

Now polish both bevels. I use #1,500-grit automotive sandpaper stuck to a flat scrap of hardwood that's about the same size as the file. Polish the bevels by stroking them with the sandpaper. Finish the outside bevels by rubbing them on a strop charged with honing compound.

Now polish the inside surface of the cutter to get a long-lasting edge. There are thin dowel-shaped oilstones (about 1/16" or 1/8" in diameter) that can do the job (one brand is TOPINCN). Or you can wrap sandpaper around a thin dowel to polish the interior, instead of an oilstone.

Sometimes beginners get a little aggressive while sharpening and make a slight hollow in the cutter's edge. Good news: If the hollow isn't extreme, the cutter will likely work fine. And if the cutter doesn't work, the cutters are inexpensive. Get another one.

ENGRAVE STRAIGHT LINES

Once the cutter is sharp, here's how to use it to engrave straight lines. It's best to work against a wooden straightedge. I like a piece of hard wood that is 1/4"

A strip of adhesive stair-tread tape holds your wooden straightedge in place while engraving.

x 2-1/2" x 12" or so. On one face of the straightedge I stick some anti-slip tape. This stuff is available from the hardware store and is used to improve traction on ladders and steps. It can be rubber-like or sandpaper-like. Both work fine – the stuff helps keep the straightedge from slipping as you work.

It's tempting to immediately begin making cuts with the grain. Hold up. With-the-grain cuts can actually be tricky, so read on.

Engraving tools cut best when used either directly across the grain or at an angle to the grain. When used like this, shallow cuts are clean and easy to steer. Cuts that are parallel to the grain can get out of control for beginners (well, they did for me).

Choosing the right wood also can help you along.

You might think that using pine, aspen or another soft wood would be the best way to learn. Nope. Instead, pick a wood with closed grain, such as tulip poplar, walnut, cherry, beech or maple. These woods have grain that is consistent in density and they cut cleanly.

Soft woods, such as white pine, require a delicate touch. Open-pored woods, such as oak and ash, can be engraved with a little practice. (Navigating the changes in density between the wood's latewood and earlywood takes a steady hand.)

I also recommend that you spray paint the board before practicing. Many

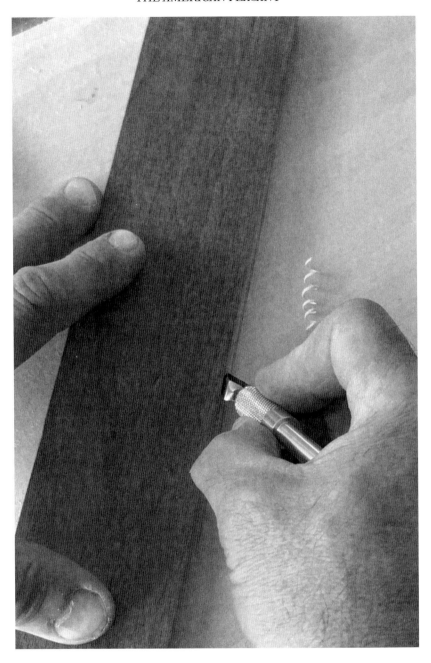

Cutting against a wooden straightedge.

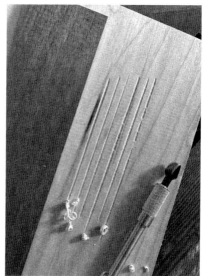

Cutting lines diagonally across the grain gives good results (usually), at left. When cutting lines parallel to the grain, several light cuts are usually better than one deep one.

of these engraving cuts are made in boards that have been painted or smoked or colored in some fashion. The paint really shows you how well (or poorly) the cut is going. Also, and this is just a gut feeling, the paint seems to make the wood a little easier to cut.

Why do I recommend spray paint? It's quick, cheap and good for practice.

So let's make a cut. Place your wooden straightedge on a piece of poplar (or whatever). Orient the straightedge so you are cutting directly across the grain. With your off-hand, press the straightedge down. With your dominant hand, hold the engraving tool with the cutter against the straightedge.

Start with the cutter nearly vertical. Pull the cutter toward you as you also gradually tip the tool toward you. As soon as the tool begins cutting, hold that angle and continue to pull the tool toward you.

Some possible problems and the solutions:

1. The line is inconsistent in width or depth. Leave the straightedge in place and go over the cut again. With a little practice, you'll learn to cut away the high spots in order to correct an inconsistent line.

2. The cut is too shallow or narrow. Repeat the cut with the tool tipped toward you a little more.

3. The cutter wanders away from the straightedge. This is an uncommon problem in cuts across the grain. But it can happen. Your cutter is likely rotated a bit so it's facing away from the straightedge. Rotate the cutter so it's par-

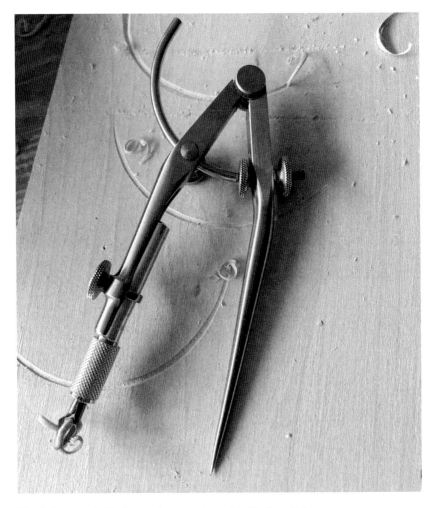

The ideal compass holds the pencil or engraving tool inside the tool's leg.

allel to the straightedge or even the tiniest bit angled toward the straightedge.

Practice with cuts 90° across the grain until you get consistent results. Now angle your straightedge so it's 30° or 45° to the grain and make some cuts. These should be almost as easy as making cuts across the grain. If you have any problems, it will be because the cutter is rotated away from the straightedge.

Then try some cuts parallel to the grain. These are the most difficult because the cutter can grab the grain at times and lift up a chip that is wider or deeper than the line you are engraving. And there's no simple way to repair or recover from those mistakes (other than making the entire line deeper).

When working parallel to the grain, begin with shallow lines until you get a feel for how that particular board is behaving. Then you can make lines with more confidence (but you should always be wary whenever working parallel to the grain).

I think you'll find that confidence helps when using the tool, like when you cut glass. Sometimes confidence is as important as skill (*see also:* playing the banjo or bongo drums).

ENGRAVE ARCS

First you need a good compass that will hold the engraving tool. Most good compasses – vintage and new – accept a pencil that is about .30" in diameter. What's important is how the compass holds the pencil.

Many cheap compasses hold the pencil on the outside of the wing/leg. These tools rarely work well for engraving.

Instead, look for a compass that has a removable steel point that can be replaced with a pencil. The pencil is gripped inside the leg of the tool, creating a stable cutting environment.

These compasses can be easily found on the used tool market. If you want to buy new, look for the C.S. Osborne Extension Divider (in 6" or 8" diameters). Or the Starrett 92. Honestly, this is a common tool that has been made for a century. I find used no-name ones for $20-$30 all the time.

In any case, don't be cheap about it. A good compass is money well spent and will serve you for many other workshop tasks (not just engraving).

The other important detail about the compass is that it should be a wing compass. This is the most common and robust form of tool. The compass locks by tightening a knob against a flat, curved piece of metal, called the wing. If the compass cannot lock securely, you will be miserable.

A 6"-diameter wing compass can handle most work, and that's the tool I recommend you start with. A bigger compass is more difficult to control, and it is necessary only for carving large chests and boxes.

USE THE COMPASS

Secure the engraving tool in the compass and set it to the desired radius. Lock the compass. Hard. Sometimes there are extra knobs on these tools that permit a little fine adjustment with the wing. Lock these down as well. Nothing on the tool should move or be loose. Any vibration or mushiness will spoil the cut or make your cut wander.

On a painted test board, press the point of the compass into the wood. Don't be shy about it. If the point moves, your cut will look a bit drunken. Don't worry about the mark left by the center point; it can be filled with paint if you're fussy. I just ignore it.

Begin the arc so you are cutting across the grain – either 90° to the grain or

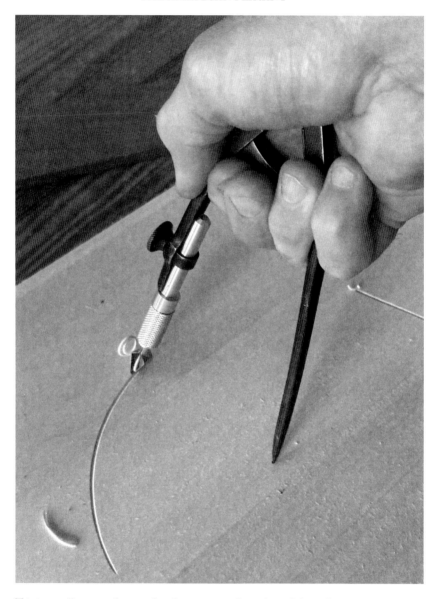

This is a small compass, but note how I am grasping the tool to stabilize it during the cut.

A Witch Mark engraved in bog oak.

Gorgeous engraving cutters made by blacksmith Tom Latane.

some other angle. Try to plan the cut so you begin cutting somewhat across the grain and end that way, too. I don't like stopping or starting parallel to the grain unless I must.

Engraving with a compass is not like drawing with one. As you begin a cut, move your fingers down by the engraving tool's cutter to push it forward there (instead of holding the tool at the pivot point at the top of the tool). This will reduce vibration and hesitation.

Begin with the cutter vertical. Tilt it forward as you begin your arc. Find its sweet spot, and the tool will make a consistent line.

Soon you will get a feel for the angle at which your cutter works best, and you will automatically tilt the tool to that angle. Practice until you can start the cut immediately as you begin rotating the compass.

Next try to make a complete circle. It isn't hard (if you've done the above exercises). And remember: You can always go over a line to even it out.

Then make a smaller circle inside that first one, using the same center point. Then a smaller one. And finally … a smaller one.

Congratulations. You just made a Witch Mark.

CHAPTER 11

GOOD WORK, AT SPEED

The following projects were built "at speed" – a term I use to describe working as fast as your hands will allow, and as slow as your stomach can bear. In other words, these projects were not fussed over like I was some author writing a book for a national audience.

Instead, they were built as if my next meal depended on the answer to the following two questions: Is this piece good enough to sell? And can I possibly afford to spend another day on this thing before I start worrying about my bank account?

Though I have built my business to the point where I don't worry about starving, there were several times during the making of this book that I had to stop myself from making another engraved coffer and had to force myself to make something salable so we didn't have to worry about a quarterly tax payment gobbling up our savings.

This is not a typical way to build stuff for a book. But it was the right way to build pieces for this book.

The furniture I love – stick chairs, vernacular chests, peasant coffers – was made by people who lived a week or two away from starvation, privation or the poorhouse. There was no time to dick around with the drip moulding on your davenport. Or obsess over ormolu on your onion-foot ottoman.

This approach can, of course, result in sloppy work. And most of the sloppy second-rate stuff ends up at the curb or in the stove.

But I have found that when I push myself – hard – to work at speed and as neatly as possible, good things happen.

The materials at hand assert themselves and play a larger part in the design process. Hmm, all the sticks I gathered are 1" thick. Am I going to shave them all down to 5/8"? If I make these drawers 6" tall, I must rip 1" off all these boards. Or I could make the drawers 7" tall and get immediately to crosscutting and dovetailing.

Also, your hands will take over operations that your brain can't deal with because there's not enough time. Give your hands a cabinet rasp and allow them to shape the comb of your chair. Sure, sketch some lines that get to a pleasing shape. But don't fuss over it with mousy strokes.

Get at it, and get it done.

The result will be something you couldn't sketch beforehand in CAD. It will bubble up deep from your subconscious, where all the chairs you've ever seen have been filed away.

It took years of work at the bench to allow myself to work this way. And that's mostly because I was surrounded by people who preferred perfection over nasty speed. Or woodworkers who stuck to the plans they had carefully drawn. Or normal people who tried to do the best job they could with a reasonable deadline.

It's rare to hear someone say: Above all, speed.

But I'm saying that to you now.

Most of the students I work with are good enough woodworkers to stop tiptoeing and simply haul ass. And when they do, their work changes for the better. It has more life. More spontaneity. And there's a lot more of it, too.

Do you think you could do this? Only one way to find out.

One of the secrets to being a successful woodworker is to have a tiny angel that lives under your left armpit that comes out to help during glue-ups.

CHAPTER 12

PRISTOLNIC

Apristolnic is Romanian seal that is used to consecrate bread for holy occasions. Typically the raw dough is shaped, then pressed with the pristolnic, which has a holy symbol carved on its underside. The honor of making this bread is typically reserved for the older women in the community.

Pristolnic can be made of wood, stone or fired clay. They come in many shapes and are typically engraved with "IC XC NIKA," which translates as "Jesus Christ's victory over death." The engraving is on the face of the pristolnic. And the base is also engraved on its underside with a mirror-image impression for the bread. The image on the base can be simple – a few words and a cross – or quite complex.

In addition to being important on holy days, pristolnic are interesting to make, paint and engrave. They are an excellent introduction to some of the shapes common in Eastern Europe's decorative objects. And they give you a place to practice engraving without risking an enormous coffer that you have spent days or weeks building.

The two pristolnic in this chapter are based on historical examples, with some liberties on my part because I am an American (we simply cannot help ourselves). If you wish to make an historical copy, you will find many examples on the internet and in books. Most of them are shaped somewhat like a Christian cross.

A plywood pattern allows you to make hundreds of copies, if you like.

OVERVIEW

These pristolnic are both made from blanks of 8/4 stock (1-3/4" thick) that are 2-3/4" wide and 8-3/8" long. The blanks are a bit bigger than required for the smaller pristolnic, so you'll have a little waste. I used black cherry for these examples, though any semi-porous hardwood will do, including beech, birch, walnut and maple.

First, you'll saw the pristolnic to shape. Then thin the top section of the pristolnic and make the pyramidal base. Clean up the saw marks, paint the pristolnic then engrave its faces and its base.

BEGIN WITH A PATTERN

Because I'm a chairmaker at heart, I first make a pattern of the pristolnic in 5mm underlayment (a cheap plywood we use to build crates here in the workshop). Patterns let me see the shape at full size and make corrections before I commit the shape to solid wood. The pattern also allows me to make multiples with ease.

Cut the plywood pattern out on the band saw and clean it up with care using rasps and sandpaper (if necessary). Then use the pattern to trace the

[128]

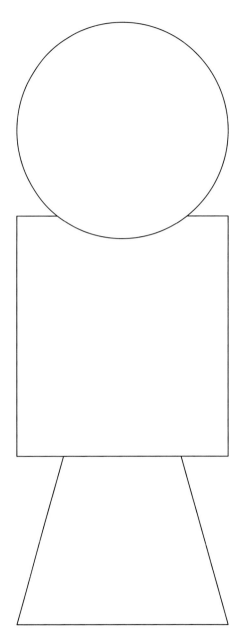

<small>Full-size pattern of the small pristolnic</small>

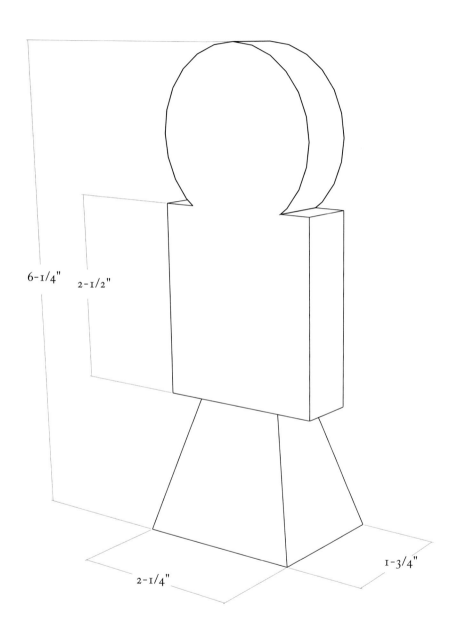

First cut the overall outline of the pristolnic.

Then use the band saw's fence to thin the top part of the pristolnic.

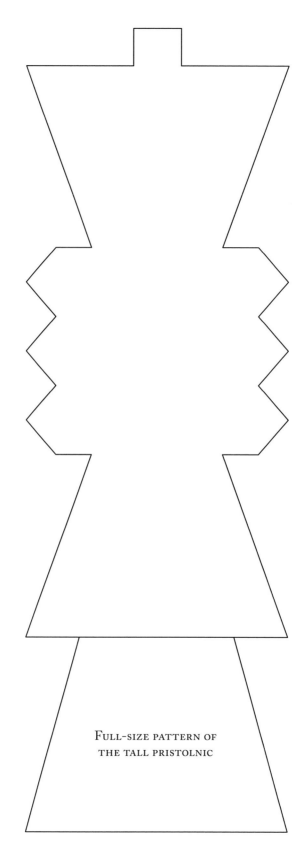

FULL-SIZE PATTERN OF
THE TALL PRISTOLNIC

Angled cuts make the pyramidal base.

shape of the pristolnic on 1-3/4"-thick stock and saw the shape. Staying close to your lines will pay off here.

Then thin the top part of the pristolnic and create the pyramidal base. I thin the top part of the pristolnic by resawing the block on the band saw with a fence. Then I cut the waste away and lay out the pyramid shape for the base. Cutting the pyramid shape is simple, leaving the rough-shaped pristolnic.

CLEAN IT UP

Once the pristolnic is roughly shaped, clean up all surfaces with a cabinet rasp, then a fine modeler's rasp. Then finish the surfaces with a card scraper. I left the edges of the pristolnic rough from the rasp. The goal here is not to make a component for a NASA rocket, but to make something that is a joy to look at and use. Focus on making the pristolnic so it feels good in the hand and looks good to your eye. Nothing more.

Break the edges with fine sandpaper. Then get ready to paint.

[133]

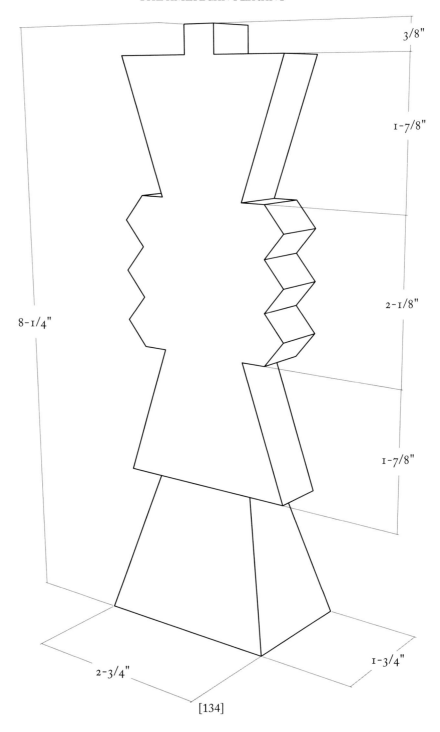

THE AMERICAN PEASANT

3/8"

1-7/8"

2-1/8"

1-7/8"

8-1/4"

2-3/4"

1-3/4"

[134]

Rasps and scrapers are all you need to clean up the faces.

PAINT THE PRISTOLNIC

You can engrave the pristolnic then paint it. Or you can paint first then engrave through the paint, which is what I did. We use a wide variety of paints here, though I prefer linseed oil paint (when I have a week to let it dry) and acrylic paint (when I have only a day).

Paint the pristolnic. When the paint is dry, you can abrade any fuzzies away with fine steel wool (if necessary) and add a second coat of paint (if necessary). In general, linseed oil paint covers in one coat. Acrylic requires two coats.

ENGRAVE

Add any symbols or ornamentation you like to the pristolnic using engraving tools. On the small pristolnic, I engraved a sun symbol at the top. The middle symbol is an evergreen tree, to symbolize eternal life. The pyramid at the base is engraved with the fishing net, a protection spell.

On the larger pristolnic, which is shaped more like a cross, I engraved a border around its edges. Then I engraved "IC XC NIKA" on the face.

The carving on the underside can be simple and done with a chisel, gouges or chip-carving tools. The typical carving I chose has the letters IC XC NIKA arranged around a cross that is surrounded by a simple border. Other seals are far more elaborate (and require more real estate to carve).

The symbol is pressed into the bread, known as prosphora, which is used as part of the Divine Liturgy (or Eucharist).

[135]

Paint, engrave then add a leather cord so people can hang their pristolnic.

The carving on the underside of the base.

CHAPTER 13

WALL RACK

I rarely take a design directly from an antique, but this was a special case. John Cornall Antiques listed a wall rack very much like this for sale in 2023. It was a 19th-century piece and was the perfect warm-up project for the complex casework later in this book.

I reduced the size of the rack a bit (the original was about 39" wide; this one is 30"). I simplified the joinery a tad and omitted a large triangular decoration in the center of the rack to make it easier to build.

The charming sawtooth decoration at the top is pretty much taken right from the original. I think it looks like flowers alternating with mountains (or wolf teeth).

OVERALL CONSTRUCTION

The frame of the rack is constructed with simple joints. The vertical stiles all have half-laps on both ends. These are glued and nailed to the three horizontal rails. The pegs are cut from a tough wood (I used elm throughout the piece) then tenoned and wedged into the assembled flat frame. The sawtooth decoration is cut with a backsaw or band saw.

The framework is painted with linseed oil paint. The pegs are wiped down with some purified linseed oil.

And the whole thing hangs on a French cleat.

A pattern makes it easy to lay out the decorative top rail (and can be used on other projects as well – it's a delightful and energetic design).

CUT THE SAWTEETH

I made a pattern to lay out the repeating sawtooth design. Affix the paper pattern to thin plywood, such as 5mm underlayment plywood. Cut out the pattern and smooth its edges. Then lay out the pattern on your top rail. Note that the pattern ends with two mountains at either end of the top rail.

Cut the sawtooth design with a series of straight saw cuts with a backsaw. I used my tenon saw, which is aggressive and cuts clean. Clean up the corners with a chisel or a knife if necessary.

HALF-LAP JOINERY

The frame is made entirely of half-lap joints. I suspect the original was all mortise-and-tenon joints. Whichever joints you use, the goal is to create a frame where all the rails and stiles are flush at the front.

To make the half-laps, first set your marking gauge to 1" and gauge the shoulders on both ends of all your stile pieces. Now set your marking gauge to the exact thickness of your rails. Transfer that measurement to the stiles, marking out the waste you need to saw away.

Saw the cheeks and shoulders of the half-laps. I used a tenon saw for the cheeks and a carcase saw for the shoulders. Clean up the work (if necessary) with a chisel, shoulder plane and/or a router plane.

[140]

WALL RACK

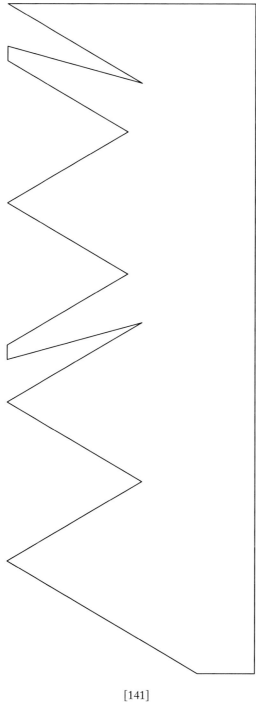

SCALE PATTERN OF THE SAWTOOTH PATTERN (ENLARGE 164 PERCENT)

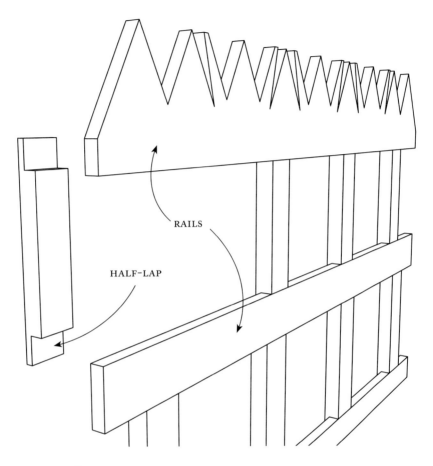

RAILS

HALF-LAP

Exploded drawing of half-laps joining the rails

Cutting list: Wall Rack

No.	Name	T	W	L
			(inches)	
1	Top rail	1/2	4-3/8	30
1	Middle rail	1/2	2	30
1	Lower rail	1/2	1-3/8	30
4	Top stiles	3/4	1-1/2	7-3/8*
4	Lower stiles	3/4	1-3/4	8*
8	Pegs	5/8	3/4	3-1/2

*1/2" x 1"-long half-lap, both ends

WALL RACK

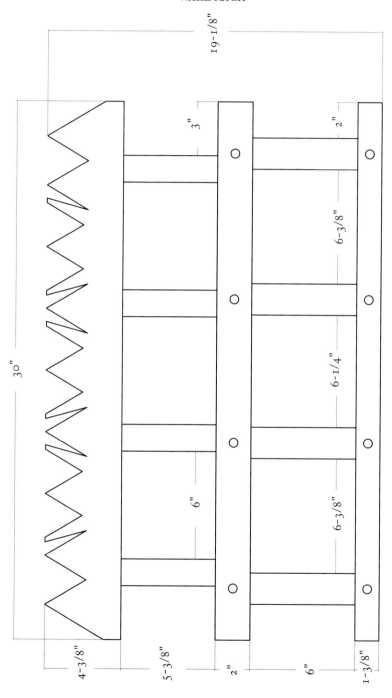

ELEVATION

[143]

With a little practice (and this project offers quite a bit) you should be able to get your half-lap joints to fit right off the saw. This one needs a little work on its cheek.

UNCONVENTIONAL ASSEMBLY

If you work with hot hide glue, assembling this rack is a cinch. Paint hot glue to a cheek of a half-lap and hold the part against its mating rail until the glue gels (it should just take only a minute). Put a clamp on the joint for extra measure. Move on to the next half-lap.

If you use yellow glue or a slow-setting liquid hide glue, you should take a different approach. Apply glue to the cheek of the half-lap and press it to its mating rail. Drive a couple pins through the rail and stile (I used a pneumatic pinner). The pins will hold the shoulder of the stile against the rail. Then put a clamp across the joint.

Here I am halfway through the assembly process. All the joints have been glued and nailed. Now I'm applying clamps across each joint to allow the glue to cure. Note the clamp applied across the top and bottom rails. This clamp was necessary to keep the shoulders tight.

Either way, clamp all the joints and let the glue cure. After the glue is dry, level off the joints of the assembled frame if necessary.

HOLES & PEGS

Drill the 1/2"-diameter holes as shown in the drawings. The exact placement isn't important. Add more if you like. Then make the pegs. Start each peg with a piece that is about 3" overlong as that will make the peg easier to hold as you work it. Saw and chisel the pegs to shape. Soften the corners with knife cuts.

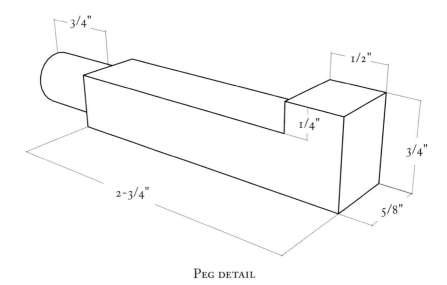

PEG DETAIL

Then cut the 1/2"-diameter x 3/4"-long tenon on the end of the peg. I used a tenon cutter in a drill. You also could use a 1/2" plug cutter or simply shave the tenon to size with a knife. To finish the peg, saw a kerf through the tenon to accept a wedge from the backside of the rack.

I finished the frame and pegs separately. We first masked off the pegs' tenons. Then we applied purified linseed oil to all the parts. Finally, we added linseed oil paint to the frame.

To assemble, glue the pegs in place and wedge them. People overload their coat racks, so the wedge is extra insurance.

Hang the rack with a French cleat. Or, if you want to be true to the original, drill some holes in the frame and hang the rack on iron nails or trenails driven into the wall.

Megan applied a coat of purified linseed oil to both the rack and pegs before painting the rack with linseed oil paint.

CHAPTER 14

HIGH CARPATHIAN WALL CABINET

Simple nailed-together wall cabinets are common in the High Carpathians (and pretty much in every rural society). In many of these cabinets the joinery is nails (or trenails) alone. I couldn't quite bring myself to do that, so there are dados and rabbets in the carcase.

In the spirit of these original peasant pieces, I made the doors asymmetrical. I simply used the boards I had on hand that also managed to cover the front of the carcase. But my favorite detail of this cabinet is the wolf teeth motif cut into the cabinet's top rail.

We currently use this cabinet in the bathroom at our fulfillment center, where we mail out all our books and tools. The wolf teeth have (so far) done a fine job of protecting the toilet paper and soap from harm.

OVERVIEW OF THE CABINET

The carcase is built with white pine. The door battens and the cabinet's catch are red oak. All the parts are nailed together (with some hide glue) with 1-1/2"-long forged nails. The backboards are merely nailed to the carcase. They have no edge joints (such as tongue-and-groove or shiplaps).

The curve on the sides of the carcase was drawn freehand. The wolf teeth on the top rail (which offer protection for the cabinet's contents) were cut with a backsaw.

The doors are kept flat with battens that are clench-nailed to the doors. And the doors are attached with iron hinges. The catch is decorative, though you can alter it to be functional if you like.

The knife line from the cutting gauge guides the backsaw as you cut the shoulder of the rabbet.

RABBETS & DADOS

Many of the projects in this book are built with tongue-and-groove joinery. This one, however, is mostly dados and rabbets. Here is how to do the job with hand tools.

The bottom ends of the side pieces have 3/4"-long x 1/4"-deep rabbets. These hold the bottom of the carcase. First lay out the rabbets using a cutting gauge. Then saw the shoulder of the joint with a carcase saw.

Use a rabbet plane (or a chisel) to hog out the waste outside the shoulder cut. The kerf left from the saw makes this an easy job.

I cleaned up the cheeks of all the rabbets with a router plane as well. You could do this with a chisel or a shoulder plane, but a router plane ensures a perfect cheek.

Cutting the dados for the cabinet's shelf and top isn't much more difficult than cutting the rabbets. First lay out the location and baselines of the dados using a knife. Then saw all the shoulders of the joints with a crosscut backsaw.

Remove the bulk of the waste with a chisel. Then clean up the joints with a router plane.

HIGH CARPATHIAN WALL CABINET

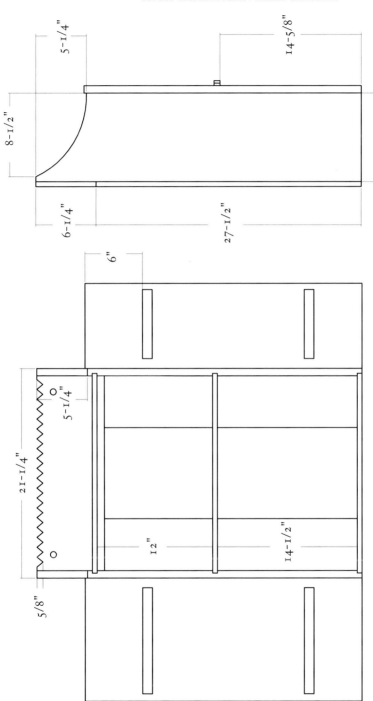

5-1/4"

14-5/8"

8-1/2"

9"

6-1/4"

27-1/2"

6"

5-1/4"

21-1/4"

12"

14-1/2"

5/8"

Elevation & profile

Straight rabbet planes are a joy to use – and are simple to sharpen.

An offcut from crosscutting the side pieces helps support the sole of the router plane. This ensures the rabbet's cheek won't slant downward, spoiling the joint.

[152]

Start sawing at the far end of the joint. Use your fingers to guide the sawplate and "nibble" back toward the other edge of the cabinet side. No need to take deep cuts – just lay in a kerf. After the kerf is established, you can saw down to the bottom of the dado.

First knock the waste out from both ends of the cabinet side using a chisel with the bevel facing up. Then remove the waste between with the same chisel – this time with the bevel facing down.

A router plane with a depth stop takes all the guesswork out of cleaning the bottoms of dados and rabbets. I set the depth stop of this router plane once and used it to clean the bottoms of all the rabbets and dados for the carcase. This ensures the case will go together square.

A CURVE & A GLUE-UP

Saw the curve on the top of the side pieces. I used a coping saw and cleaned up the cuts with a rasp. Then prepare the carcase for assembly.

First check the fit of the shelf, top and bottom. If anything needs to be planed to fit, do it now before the glue is out.

Assembly is simple. Lay one cabinet side piece down on the benchtop. Paint glue in the dados and rabbet. Drive the top and shelf into place. Then paint glue on the joints of the other side of the cabinet. Drive it into place on the shelf and top pieces. Then slide the bottom in place.

Glue all the pieces together with one of the side pieces flat atop your workbench.

Once all the sides, top, bottom and shelf are glued, apply clamps across the joints to square things up and bring the mating surfaces together for a good bond. Let the glue cure overnight. (Note: I use liquid hide glue, which cures slowly. You can work faster if you are using yellow or white glue.)

NAILS

After the glue cures, nail the top, bottom and shelf in place with tapered-shank nails. (Tapered-shank nails can be cut nails, forged nails or blacksmith-made roseheads.) The ideal length of nail for this job is 1-1/2".

If you haven't used this sort of nail before, make a practice joint to determine the correct pilot hole – both its depth and diameter. The pilot hole's dimensions vary based on the wood and the shape of the nail itself. So it's difficult to provide a lot of guidance. A couple quick test joints, however, can answer almost all your questions.

FINAL CARCASE DETAILS

An internal cleat below the top helps you to easily nail on the backboards. Glue the cleat to the underside of the top piece. Also, you can nail or screw

Three of these headed nails are enough to secure each end of the shelf, top and bottom. The blue tape helps you lay out the nails' locations only once. Then you can move the tape to the next location and skip any more measuring.

through this cleat when attaching the cabinet to a wall. I used a French cleat to hang the cabinet. The French cleat is screwed to the back through this internal cleat.

The second detail to the carcase is the top rail, which is embellished with a wolf teeth spell. The tips of the teeth are 1" apart from one another. Lay them out then cut them with a fine-tooth saw.

After you cut the teeth, glue and nail the top rail to the carcase.

The last detail is to nail the backboards to the carcase. Many of these cabinets had backboards nailed in place without any joints on their edges to accommodate wood shrinkage. I went with the authentic approach.

The teeth are fragile after you cut them, so take care.

HANG THE DOORS

Hang the doors using simple butt hinges. Cut hinge mortises for the leaves, then screw the hinges in place. After the doors are installed, you can add the battens to the doors, which help keep them flat.

Clinching the battens to the door is done with headless brads. (The headless brads have just enough of a head to keep the battens in place.) First clamp the battens to the doors. Drill pilots through the door for the brads. Set the brads in place with a hammer.

Now rest the door and battens on a steel plate (or the top of your table saw).

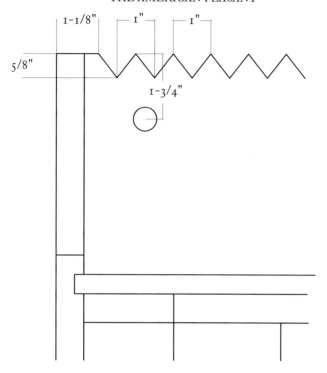

DETAIL OF THE WOLF TEETH

Cutting list: High Carpathian Wall Cabinet
(inches)

No.	Name	T	W	L	Notes
2	Sides	3/4	9	33-3/4	glued & nailed to shelves
3	Shelves	1/2	9	20-1/4	in 1/4"-deep dado or rabbet
1	Top rail	1/2	6-1/4	21-1/4	glued & nailed to carcase
	Backboards	1/2	21-1/4	27-1/2	boards butted together
1	Left door	3/4	12-1/2	28-3/4	
1	Right door	3/4	8-5/8	28-3/4	
2	Short battens	3/4	1	7	clench-nailed to door
2	Long battens	3/4	1	10-3/4	clench-nailed to door
1	Internal cleat	3/4	1	19-3/4	located under top shelf
1	Catch	1/2	5/8	2-3/4	

The butt hinges (4) shown here are from Horton Brasses, HF-30 in wrought iron – but any simple hinges will do.

CLEAT

If the backboards shrink there will be gaps between them. Should you care?

Drive the headless brads in. The tips will bounce off the steel plate and staple the batten to the door. Like magic.

With the battens in place, the rest is up to you. You can add a turnbuckle catch, paint, spells, whatever you like. Hang the cabinet with a French cleat, or use the holes in the cabinet's top rail or the internal cleat below the top.

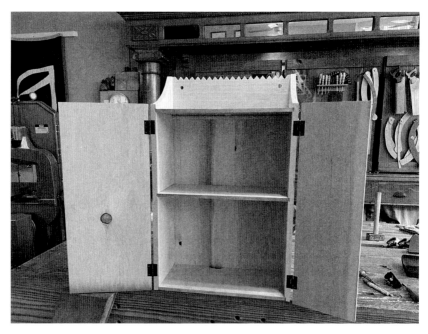

Cut the hinge gains in the doors. Then clamp the doors to the carcase and transfer the hinge-mortise locations to the cabinet with a knife. Then cut the gains in the carcase.

It's a weird photo, I know. But here you can see the brads in place as I put them on a steel "bucking plate."

CHAPTER 15

PLATE RACK

Wall-hung racks for storing and displaying crockery are another common item in peasant homes. This one is engraved with protection spells for the household (and perhaps to guard the crockery). When I first designed this rack, I drew it with wolf teeth (instead of the undulating hills shown here). But it was a bit too – bite-y. One other common motif in Carpathian furniture is undulating hills or bumps. Sometimes they are continuous, as shown here. Other times a bump or two is missing – interrupting the pattern and providing some visual punctuation.

OVERVIEW OF THE PROJECT

Like the wall cupboard, this rack is assembled with dados, nails and glue. The four shelves rest in 1/4"-deep dados. The undulating rails are attached with glue and nails. And the cleats are nailed or screwed to the back of the assembled rack.

This rack is built with tulip poplar. The exterior pieces are painted with linseed oil paint. And the entire piece is coated in purified linseed oil.

GANG-CUTTING DADOS

The dados are cut like the joints in the wall cupboard, with one exception. To ensure that all the dados line up on both side pieces, the sides are clamped together and the dados are sawn in one go.

Use the drawings to lay out the dado locations on the side pieces.

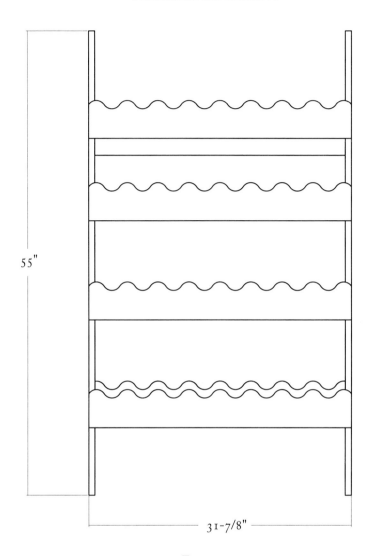

ELEVATION

PLATE RACK

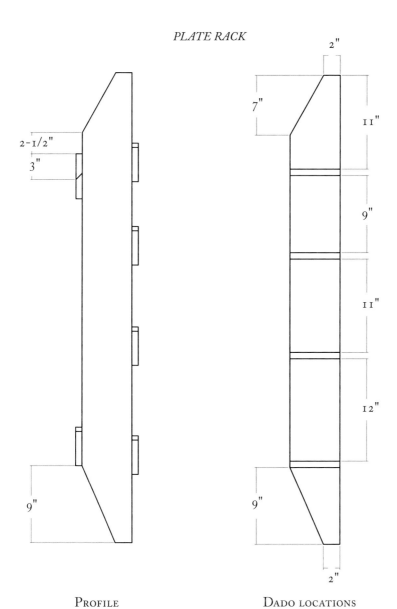

PROFILE   DADO LOCATIONS

It's easy to mess up when laying out a bunch of dados – eight in this case. By gang-cutting them, they will line up. And if you make a layout mistake, it will be the same on both side pieces, making it a minor error.

If you don't have clamps, simply nail the joints while the glue is wet. Nails usually provide enough oomph to close the joint.

Because there's a lot more wood to saw here, I use a crosscut panel saw (8 points per inch) to saw the dados' shoulders. Then remove the waste between the saw kerfs with a chisel and router plane (just like with the wall cupboard).

Saw the long decorative bevels on the ends of the side pieces. (Note that the top bevels are different than the bottom bevels.) Clean up the saw marks with a jack plane.

GLUE & NAIL

Assemble the carcase just like the wall cupboard. Put one side face up on your bench, paint glue in the dados and knock the four shelves in. Then glue the dados in the other side and knock it onto the shelves. Add clamps and push the assembly until it is square. If you don't have the clamps to do the job, nail

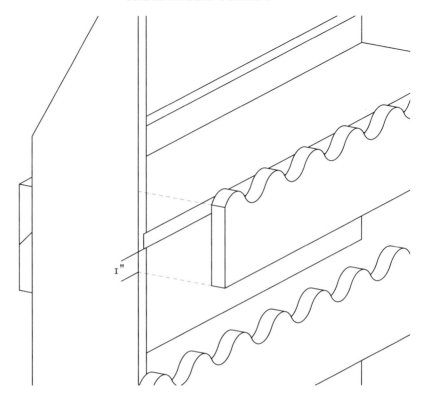

DETAIL: RAIL POSITIONS

the joints immediately while the glue is wet. I used two headed nails (4*d* or 1-1/2") per joint.

If you are able to clamp up the carcase, wait for the glue to dry, remove the clamps, then drive the nails.

THE HILLY RAILS

Make a wooden pattern of a few of the hills so you can lay out all the rails in short order. The hills are 1" high and repeat every 3-3/4". Space the hills so the pattern is centered on the rail. On a lark, I added the hill pattern to the bottom cleat.

I used a little 10" band saw to make these cuts. A coping saw or bowsaw will work if you aren't facing any crushing deadlines in your life. Clean up the cuts with a rasp and sandpaper.

Attach the hilly rails (and the hilly cleat) to the carcase. Note that the bottom edge of each rail is about 1" below the shelf it covers. First I glued the rails

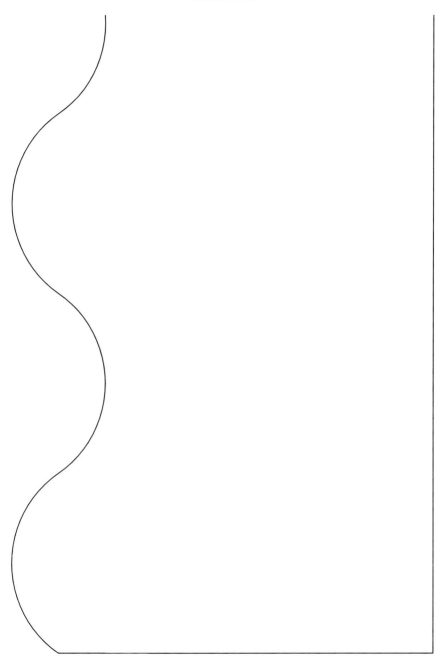

F<small>ULL-SIZE BUMP PATTERN</small>

An inexpensive band saw makes easy work of the dozens of curved bumps.

in place, then I added nails after the glue had dried. If you are short on clamps or time, add glue, then immediately drive the nails and call it done.

Clean up your work, then apply linseed oil to all surfaces. We then painted the exterior surfaces with a dark green linseed oil paint. After that dried, I engraved the spells on the front rails.

THE CLEATS

The rack hangs on the wall via a French cleat. Cut a bevel on one long edge of each cleat. Attach one cleat to the back of the carcase with glue plus nails or screws. Attach the other cleat to your wall with stout screws or (in a masonry building) masonry screws.

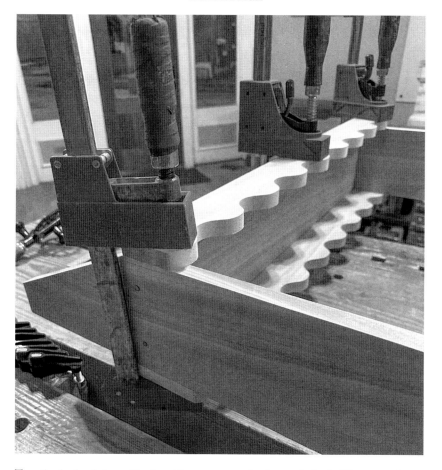

The rails, glued and clamped in place. Here you can see the cleat on the back of the carcase that also has the hills.

Cutting list: Plate Rack

(inches)

No.	Name	T	W	L
2	Sides	3/4	6	55
4	Rails	3/4	4-3/4*	31-7/8
4	Shelves	3/4	6	30-7/8
3	Cleats	3/4	3	31-7/8

*overwide to account for cutting decorative detail

CHAPTER 16

WALL CUPBOARD

This small cupboard is designed to hold small mugs and glassware. The narrow rail above the shelf helps prevent ceramics or glass from falling to the floor as you reach for another piece on the shelf.

As case pieces go, this could not be simpler. The carcase is assembled with rabbets, dados and nails. The face frame is merely glued together, then nailed to the carcase.

Several people who are familiar with this type of piece said its carcase is usually inset into an opening in a wall. You also could mount the carcase on a wall and let the entire piece stand proud of the wall.

I engraved the face frame with five fishing net protection spells – no one likes to lose their favorite mug to the cruel floor. Plus, I added front and center a general protection spell for the home.

MATERIALS

Any available softwood or hardwood is fine for this piece. I used basswood because we received an unintentional shipment of short bits of the stuff. And this piece is great for short bits. Plus you'll need some glue and some 4*d* and 6*d* nails.

RABBETS & DADOS

The only joinery in the carcase is rabbets and dados. The rabbets secure the top and bottom horizontal pieces. The dados hold the shelf.

You don't need a rabbet plane to make rabbets. For small pieces such as

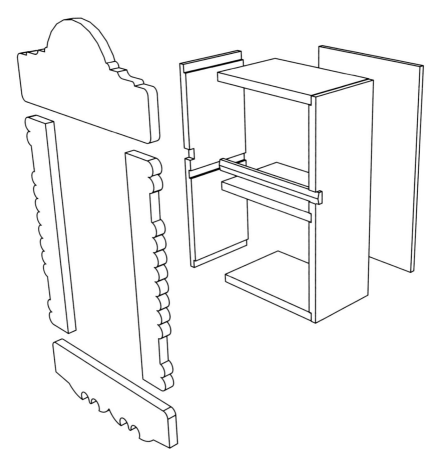

EXPLODED DRAWING OF THE CUPBOARD

this, I like to saw the wall of the rabbet then chop out the rest with a chisel. The rabbets are 3/4" wide and 1/4" deep. Use a cutting gauge to mark out the rabbets. Crosscut the wall of the rabbet. Then pop out the waste from the end-grain side of the joint. Finish truing the joint with a router plane and shoulder plane if necessary.

The dados are made in a similar way. Saw the walls of the dado to 1/4" deep. Plow out most of the waste with a chisel. Clean up the floor with a router plane if available.

WALL CUPBOARD

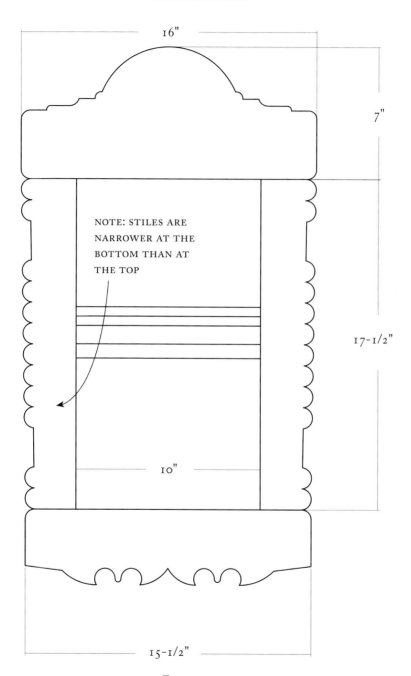

16"

7"

17-1/2"

NOTE: STILES ARE
NARROWER AT THE
BOTTOM THAN AT
THE TOP

10"

15-1/2"

ELEVATION

Sometimes a chisel and a saw are faster than setting up a moving fillister plane with its depth stop, nicker and fence.

When chiseling out dado waste, begin with the tool bevel-up. Then switch to bevel-down (as shown) once you get into the middle of the joint. And work in from both sides.

FIT THE TOP, BOTTOM & SHELF

The shelf should have a nice tight fit in its dado. If the shelf is too thick, plane the underside of the shelf. If the shelf is loose in the dado, drive a few wedges into the gap under the shelf at assembly time.

The top and bottom of the carcase just need to fit cleanly in their rabbets. True up the surfaces of the rabbets with a chisel or shoulder plane until all the pieces fit well with no gaps.

ASSEMBLE THE CARCASE

Glue is cheap, so I use it whenever I can. To join the sides to their mating pieces, first put a thin coat of glue on the end grain of the joinery surfaces. Let the glue soak in for a minute. This "sizing" of the joint makes for a better bond between the parts.

After the size coat has sat for minute, paint another coat of glue onto the mating surfaces and assemble the carcase. Clamp the pieces to hold them in place as the glue dries. Then nail the case together with 4*d* headed nails.

The back is made up of a few scrap boards that are joined with tongue-and-groove joints. To be honest, most makers of peasant pieces wouldn't have gone

I try to plane end grain as little as possible. When fitting shelves in dados, don't adjust the rabbet – that's a lot of end grain to pare. Instead, plane the underside of the shelf. You don't even have to plane the entire shelf.

to the trouble. Backboards were nailed to the back edge of the carcase without any joinery on their edges.

But I own a Lie-Nielsen No. 49, which makes both the tongue and the groove in boards that are about 1/2" thick. The plane is fun to use. It's fast. And the joint ensures gaps won't open between the backboards if the wood shrinks.

With the joints cut in the backboards, saw the boards to fit the carcase. Don't forget to leave some room for seasonal expansion and contraction, then nail the backboards to the carcase with 4*d* nails.

With the carcase assembled, true up the joints all around, especially the front edge, which joins the face frame.

AN EASY FACE FRAME

The frame is assembled with glue and nails – no real joinery. I considered joining the rails and stiles with mortise-and-tenon joints. But for a light-duty piece that hangs on the wall, it's not critical.

If you don't feel giddy when you use a tongue-and-groove plane, you might be a sociopath. Or dead. It's one of the most fun tools I own.

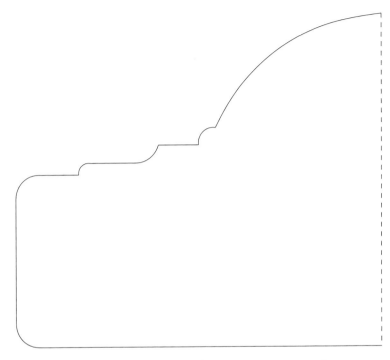

HALF OF THE TOP RAIL (ENLARGE 200 PERCENT)

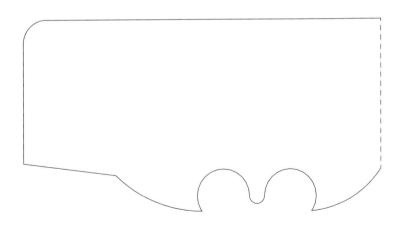

HALF OF THE BOTTOM RAIL (ENLARGE 200 PERCENT)

STILE (ENLARGE
200 PERCENT)

Long rips and crosscuts with a backsaw can
get rid of a lot of waste, clearing a path for
the coping saw (top). With a coping saw,
get as close as you can to the lines (middle).
I prefer precision over speed when sawing.
Good hand-stitched rasps make short work of
complex shapes (bottom).

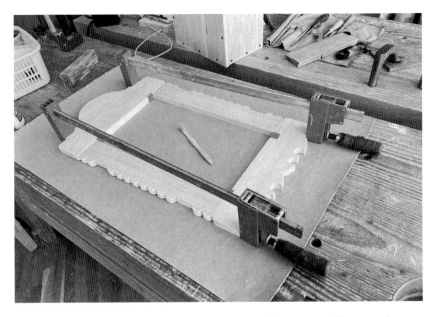

I know I'm going to some Joinery Hell (or Adhesive Heaven) for this move. Gluing up a face frame without joinery? But the carcase does all the heavy lifting with this piece.

The decorative face frame looks like a lot of work – it's not. Use a backsaw to cut out most of the waste on the top rail. Then use a backsaw to slice between the "bumps" on the stiles.

Then it comes time for the coping saw (or turning saw, if you like). I learned to do this sort of cut with the work flat on the bench. I sit in front of the bench and hold the saw vertical with two hands.

This has always worked better (for me) than holding the work vertical in a vise and sawing horizontally.

After sawing everything out, it's time to clean up the mess. Begin with a cabinet rasp. Then switch to chisels, which leave nice facets. The only sandpaper I used was to break the hard edges of the piece before finishing.

I planed a 3/16" bead on the four interior edges of the face frame to conceal any gaps between the rails and stiles.

Glue the four pieces of the face frame together. Just like when gluing the carcase, it helps to size the end grain involved in the joint.

Cut notches in the carcase for the cup rail. Saw the walls of the notches, then remove the waste with a chisel. The cup rail is beveled on its front face to catch drips of water from the glassware (just kidding; it's decorative). Plane the 1/8" x 1/2"-wide bevels with a jack plane.

Glue the cup rail to the carcase.

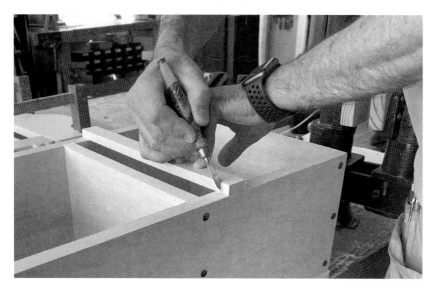

I use the cup rail to lay out the notches in the carcase. A marking knife does the job.

Another photo of things in clamps.

[183]

Last, glue the face frame to the carcase. The face frame should overhang the carcase interior by 1/4" all around the opening. Then secure the face frame with 6*d* nails.

DECORATION

The only finish is the Allbäck Holkham green linseed oil paint on the face frame. The rest of the cupboard is bare. After the linseed oil paint cures for about a week, add spells and totems to protect your collection of fine Flintstones glassware.

Cutting list: Wall Cupboard

No.	Name	T	W	L
		(inches)		
2	Case sides	3/4	7	19-1/2
3	Top, bottom & shelf	3/4	7	11
	Backboards	1/2	12	19-1/2
1	Cup rail	1/2	1	12
1	Face frame top rail	3/4	7	16
1	Face frame bottom rail	3/4	4	15-1/2
2	Face frame stiles	3/4	3	17-1/2

WALL CUPBOARD

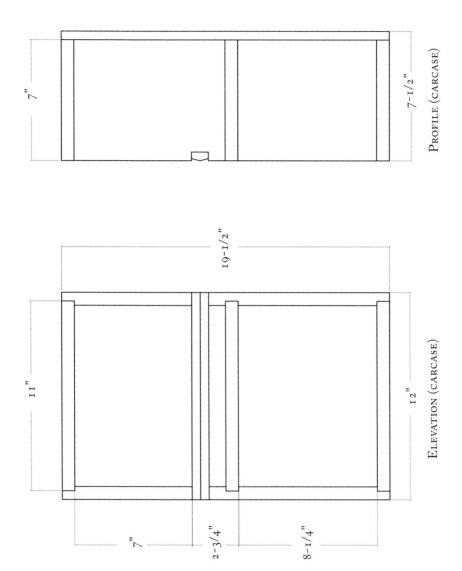

PROFILE (CARCASE)

7"

7-1/2"

19-1/2"

11"

12"

7"

2-3/4"

8-1/4"

ELEVATION (CARCASE)

CHAPTER 17

SMALL COFFER

Chests are one of the most common pieces of furniture in a peasant home – no matter where in the world it is located. When you enter a household, the family's chest is usually the most spectacular and prominent piece of furniture on hand.

Because chests are so ubiquitous, it should be no surprise that this form of furniture comes in a variety of sizes. This one is built for a desktop. It could hold all the papers and tools for running a household. Or a few treasured books. Or….

This small coffer serves as an introduction to the form. It is built almost entirely with tongue-and-groove planes. Once you build one of these small coffers, the large ones will make a lot more sense.

OVERVIEW OF CONSTRUCTION

A tongue-and-groove plane, such as the common Stanley No. 48, does most of the work. The chest has four posts. Each post is grooved. One edge is grooved to receive the rails. One face is grooved to receive the side panels.

The side panels, plus the front and back rails of the coffer, are tongued to fit into the posts. The rails are also tongued and grooved to one another. If this is confusing, study the exploded drawing.

The lid is also assembled with tongue-and-groove joinery. The ends of the lid are tongued. And the breadboards are grooved. I've made the lid a couple ways. As shown in the exploded view, the lid's tongue is created by making a rabbet on the ends of the lid. With other coffers, I tongue the ends of the lid

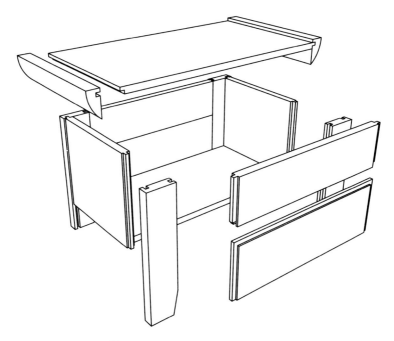

EXPLODED DRAWING OF THE COFFER

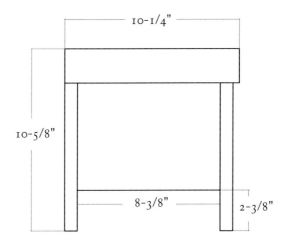

PROFILE

SMALL COFFER

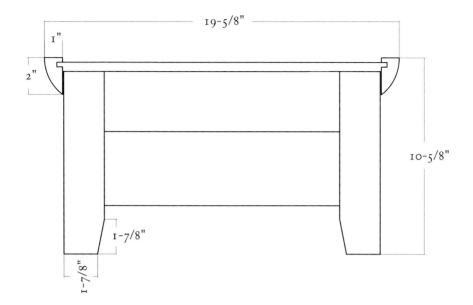

19-5/8"

1"

2"

10-5/8"

1-7/8"

1-7/8"

ELEVATION

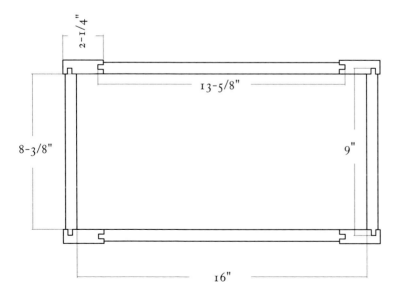

2-1/4"

13-5/8"

8-3/8"

9"

16"

PLAN (LID REMOVED)

[189]

Groove one long edge of the posts. Note the arrangement of the posts on the benchtop.

Now groove the interior face of each post as shown. These grooves receive the coffer's side panels. If you don't have a tail vise, put the post in your face vise and plane the groove with the tool turned 90° (it's easy).

[190]

Here I am cutting the tongue on a front rail. The sacrificial block, clamped to one end of the board, absorbs all the spelching and splitting from the cross-grain planing.

with a No. 49, a tongue-and-groove plane designed for 1/2"-thick stock. And then use the same plane to make a groove in the breadboards.

The lid opens and closes with the help of pegs that act as hinges. The bottom is simple. It is friction-fit to the carcase and pegged in place.

GROOVE THE POSTS

Begin by grooving the posts. First scribe a cabinetmaker's triangle on the posts so you can keep track of what needs a groove. Groove one edge of the front and back posts. Then groove a face of each post to receive the side panels.

Note that the rails and side panels are 5/8" thick; the posts are 3/4" thick. This difference in thickness makes the rails and side panels recessed in the assembled chest. To make a chest that will actually go together, you need to keep the fence of your tongue-and-groove plane running against the inside face of the rails, panels and posts.

The last detail on the posts is to add a bevel to the feet. Follow the dimensions in the drawings. Remove the material with a block plane.

Here is a front panel about to be assembled. You can see how the tongues and grooves come together to produce a complete panel.

TONGUE THE RAILS & PANELS

Here is where it gets odd. Tongue-and-groove planes weren't designed to plane end grain. But they do it just fine – as long as you clamp a sacrificial block to the outfeed side of the board so it isn't spelched or splintered off.

After cutting the tongues on the ends of each rail (it feels like work) finish the rails with the easy cuts: tongues and grooves that are parallel to the grain of the board. Then cut tongues on the side panels.

It might seem complicated to figure out which boards need tongues and which need grooves. But once you are working on the project, I promise it will be obvious.

After you have tongued and grooved all the pieces for the carcase, assembly is simple. Paint glue in the grooves and mate the posts, rails and side pieces. Clamp things up.

Here are both breadboards in one long board. Groove them at one go.

After grooving the breadboards, shape them as one piece with a jack plane. Then crosscut the shaped piece to create two (nearly) identical breadboards.

[193]

MAKE THE LID

The lid is simpler than the carcase. Cut tongues on the end of the lid, using a sacrificial board to absorb any spelching. Then groove the breadboards (if you don't have a tail vise, put the work in your face vise and rotate the plane 90°). Assemble the lid with glue. To accommodate wood movement, apply glue to only the front half of the joints for the lid. This will allow the lid to expand and contract with the changes each season.

ADD THE BOTTOM & LID

The bottom board is friction-fit into the carcase (which squares it up). Then peg it in place with bamboo skewers or 1/8"-diameter hardwood pegs.

The lid is attached to the carcase with 3/8" pegs. Place the lid on the carcase. Prop up the back edge of the lid about 3/8" using scrap. Now drill 3/8"-diameter holes for pegs through the breadboards and into the rear posts. Knock 3/8" pegs into the holes. The pegs are the hinges.

I tend to leave the pegs long so I can remove them during finishing. And I leave them long after that … just because. Someone else can trim them close; it won't be me.

After the coffer is assembled, I take it apart and paint the exterior bits with linseed oil paint. Then I carve some spells to protect whatever is going into the coffer, plus the coffer's owner.

Cutting list: Small Coffer
(inches)

No.	Name	T	W	L	Notes
4	Posts	3/4	2-1/4	9-7/8	groove to accept rails & panels
2	Top rails	5/8	3-1/4	13-5/8	5/16" TBE, 5/16" groove bottom edge
2	Bottom rails	5/8	4-5/16	13-5/8	5/16" TBE, 5/16" tongue top edge
2	Side panels	5/8	9	7-1/2	5/16" tongue, long edges
1	Bottom	1/2	8-3/8	16	
1	Lid	1/2	10-1/4	18-1/4	5/16" TBE
2	Breadboards	1	2	10-1/4	groove to accept lid

3/8" oak pegs, to act as hinges; bamboo skewers to secure bottom
TBE = tongue both ends

Put glue in the grooves and clamp the breadboards to the lid.

Secure the bottom board with small pegs drilled through the carcase and into the bottom.

CHAPTER 18

LARGE COFFER

In many ways this full-size chest is almost identical to the small coffer. Tongues and grooves abound. But because this chest is bigger, it needs tougher joinery. So in addition to the tongues and grooves, the eight panels in this chest are also joined with mortise-and-tenon joints.

These chests were usually made from riven material that was triangular in cross section (like cutting out a slice of pie). This triangular shape was exploited by the woodworker. The tip of the "pie" became a tongue. The crust of the "pie" received a groove.

I live in a dense urban area where access to green lumber is difficult. So I used sawn boards from the lumberyard (tulip poplar in this case). To imitate the look of the old chests, I made the top panels all triangular (it was a lot of work; I discuss it later in the chapter).

After assembling the chest, I realized I'd made an error. I should have made the lower panels triangular – not the top ones. Historically these chests were made this way to shed water. Because of my error, my chest has a groove facing the ceiling all around the chest. And that groove will let moisture in if it rains.

Fortunately, this chest lives inside, so the error isn't fatal. It is just stupid.

CONSTRUCTION OVERVIEW

The four posts are grooved and mortised to receive the eight panels. The panels are tenoned and tongued to fit into the posts. All the mortise-and-tenon joints are glued and drawbored.

THE AMERICAN PEASANT

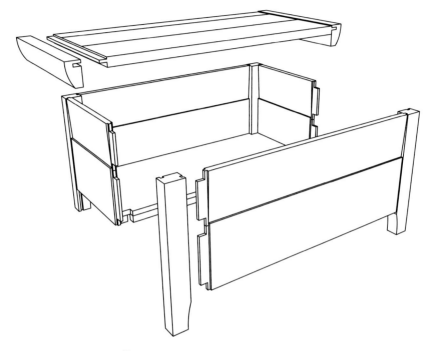

Exploded drawing of the coffer

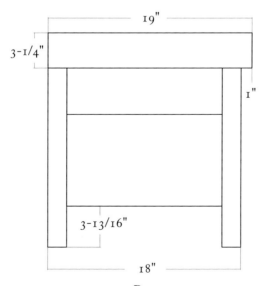

19"

3-1/4"

1"

3-13/16"

18"

Profile

[198]

LARGE COFFER

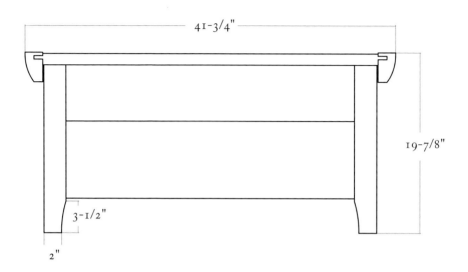

41-3/4"

19-7/8"

3-1/2"

2"

ELEVATION

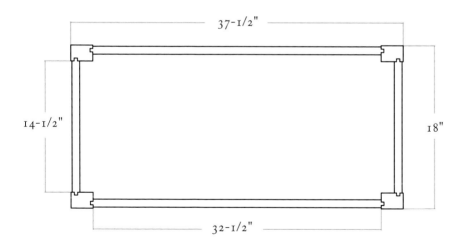

37-1/2"

14-1/2"

18"

32-1/2"

PLAN (LID REMOVED)

[199]

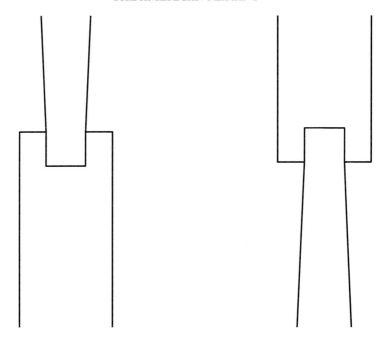

Incorrect, but OK, way to arrange the panels (left). The preferred way is at right.

The bottom of the chest rests on cleats that are nailed to the chest's interior.
The lid pieces are tenoned into the breadboard ends. Pegs and glue secure
the breadboards. The lid opens and shuts thanks to oak pegs that pass through
the breadboards and into the rear posts.

BEGIN WITH GROOVES

The grooves for the panels of this chest are 3/8" wide and 5/16" deep. Set the
fence of your plow plane so it is 3/8" from the cutter. This fence setting cuts all
the grooves in the posts. The following parts all need this groove:

1. Posts: Groove the two inside surfaces.
2. Lower panels: Groove the top edge of all four lower panels.

Then cut the 3/8"-wide x 5/16"-long tongues on the bottom edge of all the
top panels. I do this with a rabbet plane. Two rabbets make a tongue.

CUT BIG TENONS

The large tenons on this large coffer are uncommon in typical furniture making. A typical tenon for a cabinet door or face frame is somewhere between

Groove the top edge of all the lower rails (left). When the grooves are complete in the posts, it should look like what is shown at right.

1-1/2" to 3" wide. For this project, you'll rip through 6" to 8" of wood to make a tenon cheek – and do it more than 40 times to make the 20 tenons.

That sounds more like timber framing.

So your tools and your approach need to be different. I built this coffer out of poplar with some squirrelly grain. If the grain had been straight (or if I'd used straight oak or ash), then I would have simply split the tenon cheeks off the boards with a wide chisel and mallet.

If, however, you are in it for the slog, here's how to do it. Gauge in all the lines. Each tenon should be 3/8" thick and 1-1/4" long.

A tenon saw is too slow for this joint. A rip panel saw (or a full-size 26"-long handsaw) is the way to go. Controlling the saw is another matter. You can't easily saw all along 8" of end grain (well, humans can't …). So you need to saw down the edge of the board and use your kerf to guide your saw forward along the end grain.

One you have sawn out the corners of the tenon, you can focus on conquering the triangular mountain of waste between the sawn corners. A lot of hand tool dorks (myself included) are fond of saying: Just let the tool do the work.

This is not one of those cases.

You need to tell the saw to hurry the heck up. Otherwise your wrist will break off and your arm will turn to a string of hot licorice.

There are two ways to do this. First put your off-hand on top of the saw tote.

Go about halfway through the width of the board, sawing at an angle down to your shoulder. Then flip it 180° and do the same thing on the other edge.

Your off-hand adds downward pressure – making sure the teeth take a big bite. Your sawing hand keeps the tool under control. To mix things up, I'll also put my off-hand on top of the blade up by the toe. Mixing things up like this – switching back and forth – keeps you from tiring out.

Once you think you are done sawing out the waste, you probably aren't. There is usually a small hump of waste in the middle. Sometimes you can feel it by trying to rock the saw's toothline on it. No matter what, I always saw out the middle of the tenon shoulder by taking the tip of the saw's toe and using it to saw just the middle of the tenon shoulder. I might go below my baseline in the middle of the joint, but that doesn't matter.

This operation is what the saw nib was originally for. Your apprentice would hook a string over the nib to help you pull the saw forward during this difficult cut. (I KID, I KID. The saw nib was actually used to pick your teeth, lance boils and torture locusts.)

Saw out the corners of the cheek, leaving a mountain of waste between.

Now use the toothline to check your work. Put it in the kerf. It should touch your shoulder lines on both long edges. With no rocking.

To saw the shoulder, first deepen the gauge line with a wide chisel. Knock the tool's edge into the gauge line – hard. Then brace the board against a holdfast or a bench hook. Use the same wide chisel to pare a shallow trench up to the gauge line (see the photos on the following pages if this is unclear). Your saw will follow that trench.

Saw the shoulder line. The chiseled trench keeps your carcase or sash saw running true. This is my favorite part of the operation. With any luck, the cheek waste will fall away. If it doesn't, pry it off and deal with the crap in the corner between the cheek and shoulder.

Use your wide chisel to chop down any humps at the shoulder line. Then use the chisel flat on the cheek to clear off the waste. Sure, you can use a shoulder plane, but the big chisel is a satisfying way to plow the bunkus off the cheek.

You need to use downward pressure to get through these cuts. Your off-hand can provide the extra force on the handle and at the toe.

Deepen your gauge lines. First by chopping down, then pare a little waste to create a V-channel for your saw.

Saw the shoulder of the tenon. Then use a wide chisel or shoulder plane to clean the cheek.

Now saw the haunches. Leave 5/16" of the tenon at the bottom of the haunch to fit into the groove. Each haunch is 1" wide.

BASH OUT THE MORTISES

Lay out the mortises by showing the tenons to the posts. You can easily mark out the mortise locations without any measuring.

The groove will help guide your mortise chisel as you chop them out. I use the "central-V" mortising method. Start in the middle of the mortise. Knock the chisel in as deep as it will go. Remove the chisel, turn it around so the bevel faces the other direction from your first chop. Chop down right next to the first cut. The waste will get pushed out of the mortise by the back of the chisel's blade.

Repeat the process over and over, moving to the ends of the mortise. If the mortise doesn't end up deep enough, start the whole process again, beginning in the middle of the mortise.

When you are to your final depth, chop the ends of the mortise straight down, then fish out the waste.

Dry-assemble the panels, then show them to their mating posts. Mark where each mortise begins and ends on your posts.

MAKE TRIANGULAR PANELS

If you want to try your hand at making the top panels look like they were rived out, here's how I did it. I used a scorp – a tool normally used for scooping out chair seats. I took heavy cuts that got me through the job reasonably fast. Once I tapered the inside and outside faces to the tongue, I switched to a jack plane and cleaned up the furrows left by the scorp.

DRAWBORING THE JOINTS

I always prefer to drawbore my mortise-and-tenon joints if the joints are robust enough. The mechanical lock keeps the joints tight, and it reduces your need for clamps.

Before you dive into assembly, however, cut the decorative curve on the posts and clean off any ugly toolmarks.

For these joints, 5/16"-diameter oak pegs seemed about right. Begin by riving the rough pegs from a piece of dry, split oak. I use a hacking knife, but any

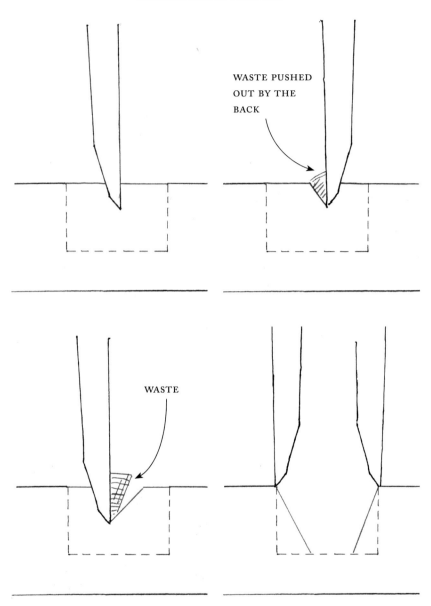

WASTE PUSHED
OUT BY THE
BACK

WASTE

With the central-V mortising method, chop, reverse the bevel of the chisel, then chop again. Reverse the bevel and repeat. The waste is ejected up the back of the chisel. Eventually you will reach your final depth with only some triangles of waste to remove at the ends of the mortise. These you chop out with the chisel vertical and the bevel facing the middle of the mortise.

Scorping the panels to taper them down to the tongue.

stout knife will do the job. Then drive the pegs through a dowel plate. Point one end of each peg like a pencil (I use a pencil sharpener). This allows the peg to navigate the offset holes.

To create the joint, first drill 5/16"-diameter holes through the posts that pass through the empty mortises. The holes should go all the way through the posts. For the top panels, I bored one hole in each tenon. For the bottom panels, two.

Then dry-assemble the joints and poke the tenons with the tip of your 5/16" drill bit. Remove the tenons and shift the point on the tenon about 1/16" toward the shoulder. Drill those holes through the tenons.

Put glue in the mortises, insert the tenons then drive the pegs through the offset holes. Saw the pegs flush on the outside of the carcase.

ADD THE BOTTOM
The bottom is simple. Nail cleats to the inside faces of the lower panels. Then plane up some tongue-and-groove boards to create a bottom. Notch the bottom boards around the posts. Then nail the bottom boards in place.

MAKE & ATTACH THE LID
The lid is a flat panel made up of a few boards that are joined at their edges with tongue-and-groove joints and glue. I also planed a small chamfer on the

Split square pegs off a block of straight-grained wood. Drive them through a doweling plate. The resulting pegs will be extremely stout and not snap as they are driven in.

Mark the hole's location on the tenon cheek using your drill bit. Then move that center point 1/16" toward the tenon's shoulder. Drill there.

Sometimes there's a gap between the hole and the peg on one side because the peg is bent. This is normal and only cosmetic.

long edges of the joints. Glue up the panel. Then cut 3/8"-thick x 1"-long tenons on both ends of the panel. I used a rabbet plane.

Cut a matching groove in the breadboard ends. I plowed this groove 3/8" from the edge of the breadboard. This made the breadboard 1/8" proud of the lid, which looks nice. Shape the breadboards.

The lid is assembled with glue and oak pegs. To accommodate wood movement, ream out the holes through the tenons toward the rear of the lid. Don't ream the ones at the front. Paint glue in the front third of the grooves. Clamp the breadboards to the lid. Drive in the oak pegs.

Finally, attach the lid to the case using 1/2" oak pegs that act as hinges. First prop up the back edge of the chest about 1/2" to 5/8", which will allow the lid to clear the carcase. Now drill 1/2" holes through the breadboards and into the posts. Drive in some 1/2" oak pegs. Don't glue the pegs in or cut them flush. You want to be able to pull them out if the chest ever needs any repairs.

FINISH & SPELLS

We painted the chest red, then I engraved a series of spells on the front of the carcase. After much thought, I decided to make the engravings the story of my childhood up until today.

Many of these peasant pieces had the bottom captured in a groove all around the inside of the case. This is a bit easier.

A rabbet plane with a skewed blade, a fence and a nicker makes this job straightforward.

Hog off most of the waste with a drawknife. Then finish with a jack plane.

AN EXAMPLE OF ENGRAVING

I didn't want to recount the story behind the engravings on each piece. I was afraid it would get too personal and perhaps embarrass someone. But because this piece is about me, and I'm beyond shame, I thought it might be interesting to hear the thought process.

I started on the legs. Straight lines are a little easier than the arcs, so they were a good warm-up exercise. The vertical dimension on this chest represents time. So I engraved the legs with the hourglass spell – a simple X in a box. There are six hourglasses. I'm 55, so I rounded up to six decades (also it would be weird for one leg to be missing an hourglass).

I separated each hourglass with horizontal bands of space. These signify – to me – that each decade of my life has been fairly distinct. The first 10 years were mostly my parents' journey – Army bases, Vietnam for my dad, medical school and finally all of us ending up in northwest Arkansas.

The second decade was filled with our family's farm. That dream died on the day my parents divorced – a shaky moment in any child's life. I got the news on a pay phone while working in South Florida.

The third decade is marriage and journalism, and the rediscovery of my childhood passion for woodworking. The fourth decade, raising kids and working at *Popular Woodworking*. The fifth decade is Lost Art Press.

Reaming the holes through the tenon near the back pushes the wood movement toward the back, where it is less visible.

There is a vertical line that runs through all the hourglasses and all the segments of my life. I call this "the bright string," and it is what pulls me forward into every new thing, from kids to starting a business to writing this book.

It doesn't have a name. But it is real.

THE LOWER PANEL

Let's start with the mountains, which are covered with the fishing net – a protection spell. These represent the fact that I cannot comfortably live anywhere flat. I grew up in the Ozarks, and the first mountain represents Wildcat Mountain where we landed in Arkansas. It was an old apple orchard and tuberculosis sanitarium.

The second mountain represents the one our farmhouse was built upon, with its beautiful view of the Boston mountains. I don't think our mountain had a name, but it was on Hilltop Lane.

The third mountain represents the seven hills that surround Cincinnati and Covington. I used to live on one of them. Now I live in their shadow. The fourth mountain is the one I have left to climb.

Above the mountains are plowed fields. These represent the farm we had, plus my parents' plans: grow strawberries, tomatoes, corn and goats. Be self-sufficient.

Amongst the fields and mountains are three engraved circles – what one reader called a BMW logo. (I can promise you I have never wished for a BMW.) They are symbols for eternal love – a reminder that I still love the mountains and my parents' failed dream.

THE TOP PANEL

It is just a big band of eternal love. This represents Lucy. If I didn't have her, this would all fall apart. She is still the first thing I think of in the morning and the last thing I think of when I go to sleep. I try not to drag her into my writing too much, but she is what keeps me going day in and out.

Though we really should sell this coffer (we need the money as this has been a rough year), Lucy really wants to keep this particular one.

I guess I just clinched (or clenched) that decision by scratching a heap of personal bullshit all over the thing.

Cutting list : Large Coffer

No.	Name	T	W	L	Notes
			(inches)		
4	Posts	1-3/4	2-1/2	18-1/2	
2	Top panels (front & back)	7/8	6-1/2	35	1-1/4" TBE
2	Lower panels (front & back)	7/8	8-1/2	35	1-1/4" TBE
2	Top side panels	7/8	6-1/2	17	1-1/4" TBE
2	Lower side panels	7/8	8-1/2	17	1-1/4" TBE
1	Lid	1-1/4	19	39-3/4	1" TBE
2	Clamps/breadboards	2	3-1/4	19	
1	Bottom	3/4	16	35-1/2	nailed to cleats
2	Short cleats	1	1	14	
2	Long cleats	1	1	32-1/2	

TBE= tenon, both ends

CHAPTER 19

CUPBOARD

These cupboards represent everything I love about vernacular forms. Everything is wrapped in tongues and grooves. Tenons hold the case together. Even the top is joined with tongue-and-groove joints. And the doors pivot on clever wooden hinges.

In short, these cupboards display all the ingenious ways that peasant woodworkers exploited the wood to its every advantage. And it's beautiful.

Design-wise, some of you might cringe at the asymmetry of the cupboard's doors. While many of these cupboards had symmetrical doors, some did not. So feel free to make the doors symmetrical. Me, I am drawn to asymmetry. In this cupboard, the difference in the door widths is a 3:4 ratio. You can experiment with different ratios, or you can simply use the damn boards on hand.

The final charming detail of this cupboard is the way the top is connected to the base: with blacksmith-made nails. There is something daring and final and confident and butt-clenching about attaching a top this way. The nails bend to accommodate wood movement. But you have to be on your A game to drive the nails without denting the top.

All in all, this project was the most fun to build for this book.

CONSTRUCTION OVERVIEW

I know this piece looks complex, but the cupboard is simple if you give it a little thought. The base is simply four frames (front, back and two sides) that are joined with mortise-and-tenon joints. In three of the frames, the frames'

<small>EXPLODED DRAWING OF THE CUPBOARD</small>

"panels" are made up of boards that are joined with tongues and grooves.

The fourth frame – facing front – has instead two doors that pivot on dowels. The holes for the dowels are bored into the frame's rails and the doors.

The cupboard's bottom and shelf are nailed in place with the help of cleats. And the top is nailed to the base.

PROCESSING THE STOCK

This cupboard is made of tulip poplar and basswood. The posts are tulip poplar, and most of the rest of the case is basswood. I split the posts out of 8/4 stock from the lumberyard. Poplar loves to split. A froe and a mallet do the job faster than any ripsaw.

After I split the posts out, I squared them with a drawknife. We don't have

CUPBOARD

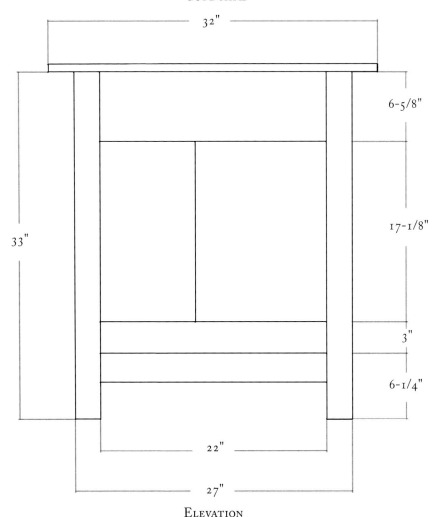

32"

6-5/8"

17-1/8"

33"

3"

6-1/4"

22"

27"

ELEVATION

space for a shavehorse in our shop, so I do this work in a clamp-on vise that raises the work above the benchtop. You don't need to make the posts square all around. Only the two inside faces, which receive the joinery, need squaring.

After the drawknife, I finish all the surfaces with a jack plane. In milder woods, such as poplar, the jack plane can leave a finished surface.

MORTISING & GROOVING

Begin work by laying out and cutting the mortises for the two front rails. They are 1/4" wide x 1-1/4" deep. Now turn to grooving for a moment. All the oth-

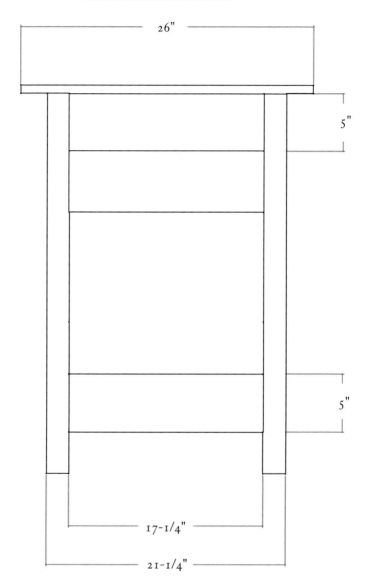

PROFILE

CUPBOARD

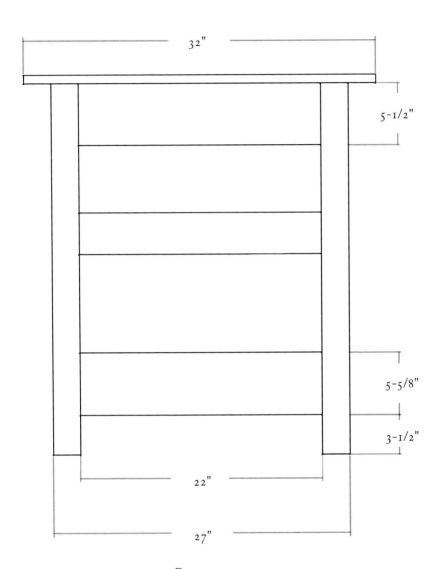

32"

5-1/2"

5-5/8"

3-1/2"

22"

27"

REAR ELEVATION

Here I am acting as a riving brake. You can control the split by levering the froe forward and back. Split off a couple pieces of scrap beforehand to get a feel for the process.

er interior-facing surfaces of the posts are grooved. Use a plow plane to make 1/4"-wide x 5/16"-deep grooves on the posts. The grooves are located 1" in from the inside corner of the posts.

Then lay out the remainder of the mortises on the posts and bash them out. These mortises are 1/4" wide x 1-1/4" deep. The mortises are in the same locations on the posts as the grooves (which is 1" in from the inside corners of the post). Cut all the mortises.

While this might be a little slower than working with a shavehorse, I like how I have access to the entire surface of the post when squaring things up with a drawknife.

BIG TENONS & THE 'TONGUE TRICK'

You can cut the tenons as shown in the previous chapter. Or, if you have a metal tongue-and-groove plane (such as the Stanley No. 48), you can try the following trick. This trick is especially useful for people who struggle to saw straight down to make tenon cheeks.

The trick is basically this: Don't start the tenon cheek with your saw. Instead, start the tenon with the Stanley or Lie-Nielsen No. 48. Make a short tongue on the end of your board. Then use the tongue to guide your saw the rest of the way down.

Here's the process: First, set your cutting gauge to lay in the tenon's shoulders on the stock. In this example, the tenon will be 1-1/4" long. Then set a cutting gauge to 5/16" (the length of the tongue) and score the ends of the tenon that would typically spelch if you planed the end grain. Score the edge grain and a little bit of the faces, too.

Now use the No. 48 to plane the end grain of the tenon. This work goes quickly. And the spelching is controlled by the little score marks you made with the cutting gauge. (Or you can clamp a sacrificial block to the outfeed side to take the spelch.)

[225]

After you plow all the grooves, lay out the mortises for the sides and back of the cupboard.

Now saw the cheeks of the tenon like you normally would. Use your off-hand to press the sawplate against the tongue. And bingo, you are right where you need to be.

Finish sawing the face cheeks. Then saw the tenon's face shoulders. I use a first-class saw cut (a la Robert Wearing) to make this easy. Deepen the shoulder mark with a wide chisel. Then pare out a triangular bit of waste to create a trench for your carcase saw to ride in.

Saw the shoulders. Then clean them up with a shoulder plane.

TONGUE & GROOVE THE FILLER BOARDS

The frame of the cupboard is done. Now you need to make the filler boards that fill in the sides and back frames. These are made with a No. 48 as well. First cut the tongues on the ends of the filler boards. Use a sacrificial block to control spelching.

Then lay out your tongues and grooves on all the long edges of the filler boards. Remember to keep the fence of your plane against the interior surfaces of the filler boards. The boards won't line up if you aren't consistent about this. (You should make this mistake only once.)

One last detail before turning to assembly: Many of these cupboards have a small stop chamfer on the top of the front posts. Make those with a drawknife.

The end of the tenon after you use the No. 48 on it.

This is like using a flush-cutting saw. Press the sawplate against the little stub of a tenon.

The end result.

Here is a top rail (below) with its mating filler board (above). You can see clearly how the tongues and grooves work together.

FIRST ASSEMBLIES

The joints in the cupboard are glued and drawbored, just like in the coffer in the previous chapter (so read that section if you need a refresher). Bore holes, make pegs and assemble the side frames first. Apply glue only to the mortise-and-tenon joints. The tongue-and-groove joints are unglued. Clamp the frame and drive your pegs through the drawbores.

A PAUSE FOR ENGRAVING

If you are going to paint over the engravings, now is a good time to engrave the front rails and the door panels. If you are going to engrave through the paint, hold off on engraving.

ADD THE DOORS

The doors swing on wooden pegs (metal hardware used to be very expensive – and sometimes still is). First fit the doors tight in the opening.

Drill 7/16"-diameter holes for the pegs. These holes are in the top and bottom of the doors and in the top and bottom rails. The holes are centered on the rails and doors and located 1-1/4" from the edges of the boards.

The stop chamfer is short and takes a few minutes to make.

Two side frames assembled.

If you are thinking about skipping the engraving, here are two quick sketches that show the cupboard with and without its spells.

The oversized door panels during engraving.

Plane off about 1/8" from the outside edge of both boards to allow the doors to pivot. Now make the four 7/16" pegs. The pegs for the bottom of the doors should be 2-1/8" long. The pegs for the top of the doors can be shorter (1-7/8" or so). Dry assemble the front frame with the doors in place.

Everything will be too tight. You need to plane off a little of the top and bottom of the doors. And maybe some material from the interior edges of the doors, too. Fuss with it until it fits.

FINAL ASSEMBLY FOR THE BASE
Then glue up the remainder of the base. Just like when gluing up the side panels, only glue the mortise-and-tenon joints. Then secure the tenons with drawbore pegs.

MAKE THE INTERIOR BITS
The shelf and bottom of the cupboard are nailed to cleats, which are nailed to the interior of the carcase. Nail the cleats in place. Then make the shelf and bottom. In the spirit of this tradition, all the boards are tongued and grooved (and glued).

You'll need to notch the shelf and bottom around the posts. Then nail these panels in place to their cleats.

Begin with the doors fit tight to the frame (left). Drill the 7/16" holes 1-1/4" from the edges of the boards. These holes are 1" deep (right).

THE TOP

The top couldn't be simpler. It's a panel made of boards that have been (surprise) tongued and grooved and glued. Assemble the panel, clean it up and nail it to the posts below. I used 6*d* roseheads made by a blacksmith. You could also use wooden pegs. The last thing I added was a latch that holds the doors closed. It is simply two pieces of oak, plus a peg that passes through the top rail of the carcase.

The pivot hinges ready to be installed in the front frame.

After the carcase is glued up, carve the spells on the posts.

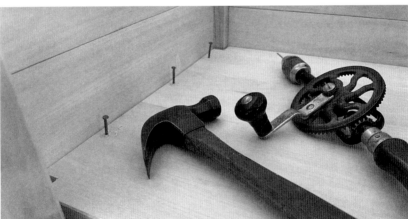

Nailed-in cleats (top) support nailed-in shelves (below).

Cutting list: Cupboard

| | | | (inches) | | |
No.	Name	T	W	L	Notes
4	Posts	2	2-1/2	33	
2	Top rails, sides	3/4	5	19-3/4	1-1/4" TBE, 5/16" groove one edge
2	Bottom rails, sides	3/4	5-5/16	19-3/4	1-1/4" TBE, 5/16" tongue one edge
	Filler boards, sides	3/4	random	17-7/8	5/16" Tongue, both ends
					5/16" T&G on edges
1	Top rail, front	3/4	6-5/8	24-1/2	1-1/4" TBE
1	Bottom rail, front	3/4	3	24-1/2	1-1/4" TBE
1	Left door	3/4	9-1/4	17-1/8	
1	Right door	3/4	12-3/4	17-1/8	
1	Top rail, back	3/4	5-1/2	24-1/2	1-1/4" TBE, 5/16" groove one edge
1	Bottom rail, back	3/4	5-7/8	24-1/2	1-1/4" TBE, 5/16" tongue one edge
	Filler boards, back	3/4	random	22-5/8	5/16" Tongue, both ends
					5/16" T&G on edges
1	Top	3/4	26	32	
4	Shelf/bottom cleats	3/4	3/4	17	Nailed to filler boards
1	Bottom	3/4	18-3/4	23-3/4	3/4" x 3/4" notches, all corners
1	Shelf	3/4	17-1/2	23-3/4	3/4" x 3/4" notches, rear corners
2	Latch pieces	3/4	1-1/2	4	
1	Pivot hinges	7/16" dowel			

TBE= tenon, both ends

T&G = tongue and groove

CHAPTER 20

PEASANT CHAIR

Τhis simple chair takes design cues from a variety of cultures that have cross-pollinated during the centuries. These cultures all faced similar problems, including this: "How can I make a chair using a minimum number of tools, a small amount of raw material and hands that are not professionally trained?"

Many cultures came up with similar solutions. This chair explores several of those ideas.

CONSTRUCTION OVERVIEW

Let's start at the bottom of the chair with the legs. The legs are the only component of this chair that uses thick material. The rest of the chair can be made with thin material, which is more readily available.

The legs are 1-3/4" x 1-3/4" x 20" and are rived from any common and strong ring-porous wood, such as oak or ash. Because they are rived, they are incredibly strong, so the chair doesn't require stretchers. Stretchers complicate the construction, and they make a chair more trouble to repair if a leg breaks or becomes loose.

The tenons on the leg are 1" diameter x 3" long and are cylindrical. To make the tenons, you can rive away most of the waste for starters and finish it with a knife or rasp. I have a lathe, so I took that path.

The seat is 1" thick, and the area around the tenons for the legs is thicker thanks to two 1"-thick battens. These battens are nailed cross-grain to the underside of the seat. Nails bend and will allow some wood movement. This

type of seat construction appears throughout Europe and even in the U.K. Most people think of it as particular to the Germans or Swiss, but you will find it almost anywhere you look.

The four legs all have the same rake and splay. This makes them easy to drill with just one sliding bevel locked to one setting – you just tilt and drill.

The seat isn't saddled, and that's OK. Most of these vernacular chairs had flat seats that tilted back a few degrees for comfort. If you need more cushion for your tush, I recommend the traditional solution: a sheepskin (IKEA sells them for about $40).

Above the seat you have a bunch of sticks, arms and backrests. It looks complicated to execute. It's not. Woodworker Rudy Everts, an artist, friend and woodworker outside Munich, and I have come up with a way to drill these angled mortises without jigs or special skills. All you'll need are a 5/8" drill bit and a sliding bevel to guide you.

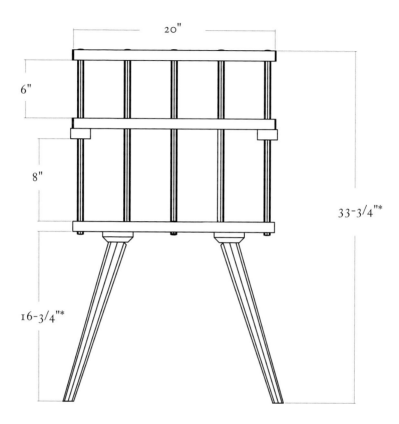

ELEVATION (*AFTER TRIMMING FEET)

The arms and backrests are cut from solid 1"-thick oak – no steambending. And the sticks can be made from 5/8"-diameter straight-grain oak dowels from the home center. I shaved mine out from 3/4" x 3/4" material. Wedges and glue hold the joints together.

This is, hands-down, the easiest armchair I've ever built. And it is surprisingly comfortable for something that resembles a box on legs.

If you find any aspect of this project difficult or confusing, you can read one of my other titles, "The Stick Chair Book" (Lost Art Press). It dives deeper into all aspects of chairmaking, and it is a free download from the Lost Art Press website.

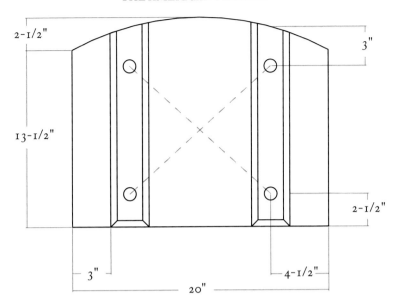

UNDERSIDE OF SEAT

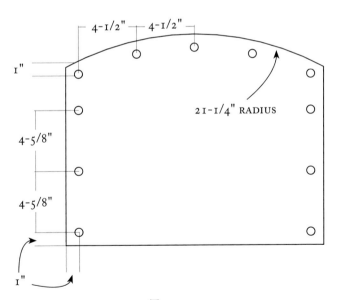

TOPSIDE OF SEAT

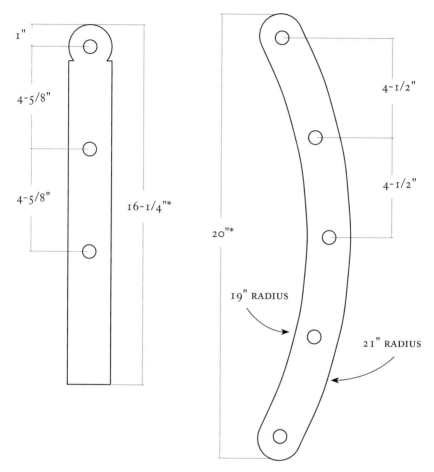

1"

4-5/8"

4-5/8"

16-1/4"*

4-1/2"

4-1/2"

20"*

19" RADIUS

21" RADIUS

ARM & BACKREST (*AFTER TRIMMING)

SPLIT & SHAPE THE LEGS

You can saw or rive the legs from straight-grained oak or ash. I bought kiln-dried red oak and looked on the edge of each board to ensure the grain was straight (look to the medullary rays, which look like silvery snakes swimming in the grain. They should be vertical along the length of the edge).

Then use a froe to split off the legs. The first split with the froe finds the true grain direction in the board. Then split off square legs. Then square up the legs however you like, with a drawknife, hatchet or machinery.

Now octagonalize the legs. The photos explain how to lay out an equilateral octagon with ease. Then you just have to handplane down the corners to the lines. I use a jack plane for speed.

A froe and mallet make short work of the legs.

After octagonalizing the legs, taper them to 1" at the foot. Simply draw a line 3/8" in from each facet on the foot. Those eight facets are your target. Taper the legs to those lines with a jack plane.

Finally, turn the 1"-diameter x 3"-long tenon on each of the legs. Or split and shave the tenons if you don't have a lathe.

JOIN THE SEAT & BATTENS

Cut the seat and battens to size. Plane a 1/2" x 1/2" bevel on the front edge and long edges of each batten. Then nail the battens to the underside of the seat. Use the drawings as a guide.

I used 1-1/2"-long forged nails. Tapered-shank nails need a pilot hole – especially in oak. So experiment with different pilot holes before you commit.

Draw a single line from corner to corner on the end grain of the leg. Set a combination square against an adjacent corner. Extend its blade to touch the line. Then use the square with that setting to scribe lines on all four faces of the leg.

I turned the tenons on the lathe with a carbide turning tool and a bedan sizing tool.

Drive in the nails and make sure to stay clear of where you will drill the mortises for the legs.

The battens will be a little proud of the seat at the back. Saw them off close to the back edge of the seat and plane them flush.

DRILL THE LEG MORTISES

Mark out the locations of the mortises on the battens. Draw an X that joins the mortises. This X represents your "sightline." This is the line that you'll put your sliding bevel on as you drill the mortises.

You're going to drill through the battens and the seat, so you need to protect the seat from spelching on the exit hole. I clamp the seat to a thin piece of plywood and clamp all that to my benchtop.

Set a sliding bevel to 23° and place it on a sightline and near one of the mortises. Basically, you want to line up your drill bit with the blade of the sliding bevel and follow that. That's it. Drill, check your angle and adjust. Drill deeper and repeat.

If you have a construction laser you can place it on the sightline as well to help guide your drilling. But a laser is not necessary equipment.

Nail the battens to the seat. You could use a sliding dovetail for this, which many old chairs did. But the nails work great.

Here is how I drill the mortises. The laser and sliding bevel sit on the X – the sightline. I do my best to follow the laser and the blade of the bevel as I drill.

DRILL THE ARMS & BACKREST

The idea for this technique first came from Rudy. He suggested that the mortises in a chair's arm, backrest and seat could be drilled by stacking the parts together and drilling them all at one time.

I've experimented with this technique for a couple years. But it wasn't until I built this chair that I tried to use it for all the joinery between the seat, sticks, backrest and arm.

It works remarkably well, and it eliminates a lot of the jigs, lasers and (frankly) skills needed to make a basic chair. The technique has limitations. But this chapter is about getting you through the construction of this chair – not contemplating how a simple technique could be used to change the world.

Put the seat on the workbench. Put one of the backrests on the seat with its rear edge flush to the rear edge of the seat. Trace the shape of the backrest onto the seat in pencil. Place the second backrest on top of the first. Flush them up.

Set your sliding bevel to the desired back tilt (12° in this case). Place the sliding bevel on the seat. Put the tool's blade so it is on the pencil line you traced for the front edge of the backrest. The blade should push both backrests back a bit. Flush up the two backrests against the bevel of the sliding bevel.

Note how the two backrest pieces are pushed backward to match the blade of the sliding bevel.

Check the angle at a few locations on the stack of parts.

Clamp the arms below the seat, flush to the outside edges of the seat. The arms are overlong, so their exact position forward/back isn't critical. Just get them flush to the left and right edges of the seat.

Clamp the stack of parts to the seat. Then clamp the seat to your workbench with the back of the seat hanging off your workbench (so you don't drill into your workbench).

DRILL THE MORTISES FOR THE BACK

Drill the mortises for the sticks through the backrests, seat and arms all in one go. I used a Star-M bit (16mm or about 5/8") for this. It doesn't splinter on the exit side of the hole. Tilt the drill bit at 12° and use the sliding bevel to guide your drilling. Note that you are tilting straight back for each hole in relationship to the front edge of the seat. Don't tilt straight back relative to the curved rear edge of the seat in this example. (In other words, use a 0° sightline for these holes.)

After drilling the mortises, release the clamps.

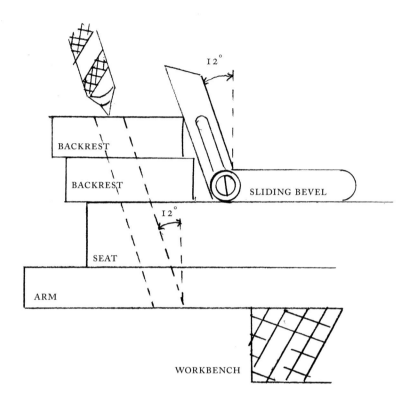

BACKREST

BACKREST

SLIDING BEVEL

12°

12°

SEAT

ARM

WORKBENCH

STACKING PARTS FOR DRILLING

ASSEMBLE A BACKREST & ARM

Take a scrap 5/8" dowel. Thread the arm and the backrest on the dowel, then place the dowel in one of the corner mortises in the seat. Slide the backrest and arm upward so the bottom of the arm is 8" off the seat.

Now you need to measure how far back the backrest is with these components at 8" off the seat.

Place a try square on the seat with its blade on the pencil line you traced there earlier. Now measure the distance between the blade of the square and the backrest. In our case it was 1-5/8". That's how much the backrest moves back at 12° and 9" off the seat.

Disassemble the dowel, backrest and arm.

Here is some visual rise-and-run. The combination square shows the height of the backrest and arm. The 6" rule shows how much the parts have shifted back when 8" above the seat.

POSITION THE ARMS FOR DRILLING

Place the arms on top of the seat. Line up the through-mortises in the seat with the mortises through each arm. Make a tick mark on the arm and seat, marking this position. Now slide the arms backward 1-5/8" and clamp them to the seat.

Lay out and drill the through-mortises for the short sticks through the arms and the seat.

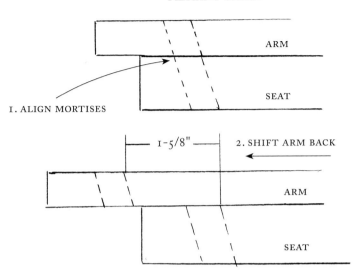

1. ALIGN MORTISES

ARM

SEAT

⊢— 1-5/8" —⊣   2. SHIFT ARM BACK

ARM

SEAT

SHIFT THE ARM BEFORE DRILLING THE SHORT STICKS

Drill the mortises for the short sticks straight down.

[249]

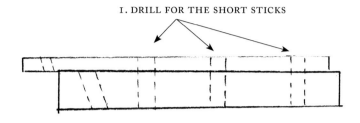

1. DRILL FOR THE SHORT STICKS

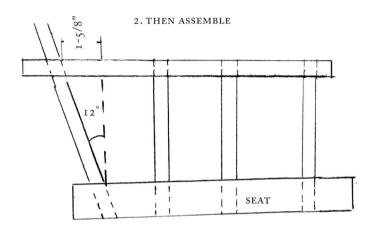

2. THEN ASSEMBLE

THE SEAT, BACK & ARM

ASSEMBLE THE UNDERCARRIAGE

First cut some kerfs in the tenons of the legs to make it easy to get some wedges in there. Now join the legs and seat. Paint the mortises and tenons with glue. Drive the legs in until each tenon shoulder hits a batten.

After the four legs are seated, turn the assembly over. Paint glue on each wedge and drive it into the kerf in each tenon. Let the glue dry overnight. Then saw the tenons flush to the seat.

MAKE THE STICKS

If this is your first chair, make it easy on yourself and buy some 5/8" oak dowels from your local hardware store. These will work fine and make a strong chair. If you are a chairmaker already or a glutton for punishment (I'm a card-carrying member of that club), then make your sticks from scratch.

I saw or rive them out from straight-grain oak. Then I work them into 3/4" x 3/4" octagons. I cut 5/8"-diameter tenons on their ends then shave the

Wedges with dead-straight grain can be driven like a steel nail.

octagonal part down to the round part.

The short sticks are overlong with 2-1/4"-long tenons on both ends. After making each stick, trim it to fit its mortises. Cut kerfs in the tops of both the short sticks and the long sticks to receive wedges.

LEVEL THE LEGS

Before assembling the arms, backrests and sticks, this is a good time to cut down the legs so the seat tilts back a bit (3/4"). First place the chair's base on a level surface. Level the seat using a level and small wedges under the legs.

Once the seat is level, place 3/4"-thick blocks under the front legs. This sets the tilt of the seat. Finally, drop a ruler from the front edge of the seat to the final seat height you desire. I used 16-3/4". Set a scribing tool so its pencil touches the tip of the ruler. Use the scribing tool to mark all the facets of the four legs.

After the legs are marked, saw the legs to final length, following the pencil lines from the scribing tool.

SHAPE EVERYTHING

Now use rasps and sandpaper to shape the arms and backrests to shape. This is your opportunity to shape things to your liking. Most vernacular chairs used simple arcs and lines, but this is your chair.

[251]

A 3/4" x 3/4" short stick and a Veritas 5/8" Power Tenon Cutter. I make more than 1,000 sticks in a year for classes and the chairs I build, so this process is automatic.

For the long back sticks I use this Ray Iles 5/8" rounding plane to shape the majority of the stick. Then I plane the rest of it with a block plane until I get to the desired shape.

I shape my sticks mostly with a block plane and a jack plane. I work against a stop in a vise. No need for a shaving horse or a drawknife.

The front legs are propped up 3/4". The cabinet scribing tool is set to mark the legs all around.

[253]

Follow the pencil lines to saw the legs to length.

I have glued up a lot of stick chairs during the last 20 years. And there are defi-nitely good and stupid ways to do it. I've done them all. Here's the best way to get through it without a broken arm or backrest.

First glue a long stick into its mortise in the corner of the seat. Knock it home with a mallet. Now glue the short sticks into the arm for that side of the chair. Put glue on both the mortise and the tenon. Rotate the stick so the kerf is perpendicular to the grain in the arm (to prevent splitting the arm).

Slide the arm and short sticks over the long sticks. Glue the short sticks into the seat. Knock the arm until it is 8" above the seat. Repeat this process for the other side of the seat.

With both arms and the short sticks glued in place, you can deal with the long sticks. First slide the lower backrest onto the back sticks. Push it until it rests on the arms.

Now put the top backrest onto the long back sticks. Position it until it is comfortable for you. I have long torso, so I put the top backrest 6" above the lower backrest. Yours might be lower.

Once you find the best position for the top backrest, you can trim the long sticks and wedge the top backrest in place.

The chair is essentially done. Let the glue dry, cut all the tenons flush and clean up the chair.

I used scrap wood (6" wide) to keep the top backrest from sliding down as I wedged it in place. Might be overkill.

Cutting list: Peasant Chair
(inches)

No.	Name	T	W	L	Notes
1	Seat	1	16	20	
2	Battens	1	3	16	1/2" bevel, three edges
4	Legs	1-3/4	1-3/4	19	1" x 3" TOE
2	Arms	1	2	18	overlong, cut to fit
2	Backrests	1	4-1/4	21	overlong
5	Back sticks	5/8 dia.		20	2-1/2" TOE, overlong
6	Short sticks	5/8 dia.		12-1/2	2-1/2" TBE, overlong

TOE= tenon one end
TBE= tenon both ends

St. Louis in 1874 B.S. (Before Schwarz.)

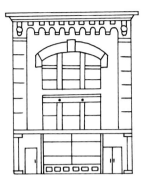

CHAPTER 21

THE URBAN PEASANTS

I never got to ask my parents why they sought to be homesteaders with a farm in the middle of nowhere in a house built entirely by their hands. But my grandfather Schwarz – Popo, as his grandchildren called him – gave me a few clues.

At the end of his life, Popo lived alone in a retirement village that had been built on the site of our town's tuberculosis sanitarium. I'd visit him when I returned home from college, and like many people near the end of their lives, his past was far more present than his present.

Sometimes he'd open a box of things and tell a story about them. Popo had worked in a paper factory, but he also did a stint as a freelance photographer. And he had kept a photo he had taken after a devastating tornado in St. Louis.

In the boxes were documents in other languages.

Yes, our name is German, he explained once. But that's not the whole story. The family had lived in Ukraine for many years, then briefly in Switzerland before emigrating to the U.S., about 1910. They landed in the Dakotas and made bricks.

"They made bricks?" I asked.

Bricks.

Eventually they made their way to St. Louis, which is where Popo grew up, and my dad and I were born. After making bricks, the Schwarz family managed to buy a house in Lafayette Square, a neighborhood that had been in decline since a tornado in 1896. They opened a boarding house where the whole family lived and worked.

They were, for lack of a better word, urban peasants.

My father, however, was a striver. The first Schwarz to ever graduate college. But after he had climbed as high as he could (he was a medical doctor), he and my mom bought 84.4 acres in the middle of nowhere in Northwest Arkansas.

The farm never quite worked out. We built two homes on the land and almost finished the second one. But then my parents split. I fled to the biggest city that would have me, Chicago. After a brief stint as a newspaper reporter, I became a low-level magazine editor at *Popular Woodworking* magazine. Then, after years of loving my job while hating my bosses, I began to repeat the cycle begun by Gustav Schwarz, my great grandfather.

First, I quit my job. Then, like Gustav, I looked to declining neighborhoods in the inner city for a place to live and work. Why? It was the only place where I could afford what I wanted: a workshop with living quarters above.

When I began my years-long search for a building, I walked the dense 19th-century neighborhoods of Covington, Kentucky, in the early morning or after our kids went to bed.

Searching for real estate at odd times taught me a couple things.

1. City neighborhoods are different in the evenings. Places that are quiet in the day are bonkers in the evening when people are home from work and relaxing on the porches, sidewalks and in city parks. Talking to their neighbors, playing ball in the street, yelling at streetlights. It's energizing and very unlike the suburbs.

2. When the sun sets, and the interior lights flick on, you can see how our cities have been ruined. And you can see their almost unlimited potential – perhaps an answer for some American peasants.

I first realized this when I walked up Madison Avenue – the main street in Covington – after dark. All the storefronts were lit up. But the second, third, fourth and fifth floors of almost all the buildings were dark. In fact, if you didn't know that you were walking among tall buildings, the ground-floor lighting could trick you into thinking you were walking in a low-rise suburban shopping center.

When I walked the same streets the next morning, I began looking at the buildings a bit differently. I started to peer above the ground floors and into the windows above. What was behind the glass? Living space? Storage? An empty void?

I got my answer a few weeks later. A real estate agent wanted to show me a new development on Scott Boulevard. They were transforming an old building into a series of condos, and they would be willing to build one unit to suit my work, with a ground-floor storefront/workshop and living space above. Price, about $350,000 when completely finished. With parking.

Would we be interested?

That was entirely more than we could afford at the time, but I desperately

STADT PFARRKIRCHE ZU U. L. FRAU IN MÜNCHEN.

From Popo's papers. I'll never get to ask him if Munich is part of the family story.

wanted to see the inside of the building. So I took my youngest, Katherine, with me after school one day, and we met the real estate agent at the back door of the building.

Very little new work had been done on the structure. So Katherine and I explored this intact older building – about 20,000 square feet of it. It was like using a time machine. There were apartments with original fixtures, mantels, mouldings and architectural details. The plaster wasn't perfect, but the units weren't in bad shape.

Half of the structure had originally been offices. And again, it was like walking onto a movie set from the 1930s. There were endless hallways with offices behind frosted glass with people's names and departments hand-painted on the doorways. All the architectural details were undisturbed. It was just a little sloppy and dusty, with old electric and plumbing.

In our old central cities and small towns, there is a world above every ground-floor retail establishment. For hundreds of years, people lived above the stores they owned. Or they lived above other people's stores. It wasn't that long ago. And when these people left for the suburbs, a lot of these places were sealed up and forgotten.

The barroom at our workshop on Willard Street in Covington, 2015.

I know of about a dozen Covington buildings that are veritable time cap-sules, just waiting for someone to reclaim the unused space above the first floor. Hell, we bought one of these buildings in April 2023 to create a fulfill-ment center for our publishing business. It still had a working line shaft, an original toilet and a metal rack with all the employee's timecards. Little about the building had been significantly altered in 130 years.

But here's the odd thing: These places don't show up in traditional real estate listings. I found out from a neighbor that the building might be for sale. These places are not considered livable by most people because they need new elec-tric, plumbing and plaster (for starters). And they aren't stand-alone houses on patches of land. They are these weirdly gorgeous spaces that are difficult to isolate and sell. Maybe they should become businesses. Or boardinghouses run by German-Swiss-Ukrainian brickmakers.

Oh, and no one wants to insure these buildings – I've had three policies canceled, even though I've never filed a single claim in 34 years of ownership. And the county building inspectors have no idea what to do with you, so some of them make your life as difficult as possible. Making an old building meet modern code is no small thing. Old buildings were built with a different set of goals.

But it's not all grumbling and despair.

During the summer, Lucy and I like to go for walks in Covington after the sun has gone down and the temperature has dropped a bit. Even though 12 years have passed since my first journeys into the Covington wilderness, little has changed when it comes to seeing life above the ground floor. Sure, a few buildings have become apartments that are lit from within. But there is room here for literally thousands more people.

In 1930, Covington had 65,252 residents (and it had far smaller borders then). Today, its population is 40,837. So please bring 25,000 of your closest friends to town – we have room to spare.

And Covington isn't an anomaly. Go to any Southern or Midwestern town with a cluster of tall buildings. Wait for sundown. The lights will flicker on – on the first floor. Above is darkness. An opportunity to create your own village, your own workshop.

Lucy and I did it. The process sucked, to be honest. But right now I'm sit-ting on the second floor of our building with a nice fire burning. The cats are lying flat out in front of it on a sheepskin, the lazy bastards. Outside the sun is setting over the steeply pitched roofs and bell towers that surround us, turn-ing everything orange.

We might go out for a drink. We might walk to the river to see the old city bridge all lit up. Or we might just stay by the fire (the cats will approve) and enjoy the quiet life of American peasants.

APPENDIX 1

OTHER PEASANTS

Though the projects in this book are rooted in Eastern and Central Europe, I have been surprised by the similarities between the Eastern European pieces and the rural forms of furniture in Sweden, Norway, Germany, Austria and Denmark.

This chapter contains photos of rural furniture from two open-air museums: Skansen, on the island Djurgården in Stockholm; and Frilandsmuseet, which is outside Copenhagen, Denmark.

Both museums are filled with objects from all over Europe – not just Sweden and Denmark.

I hope these images open your eyes to other forms you can build using the methods outlined in this book. And that they remind you to visit every museum you can on your travels.

A low chair that folds out to become a table. In Swedish: Fällstol.

Backstools (and regular stools) were some of the most common forms of seating in rural Europe.

Another convertible chair/table.

An unusual (and difficult to photograph) backstool with a wishbone-shaped back.

A bench with a hinged back. The back flips over the center post, turning the sitter from the table to the room.

Three-legged stools are ubiquitous in farmhouses.

A delightful stool made with square mortise-and-tenon joinery.

Note how the bark at the rear of the stool creates an underbevel.

A simple, but charming, framed bed.

Woodenware, much of it decoratively carved, is displayed in racks.

Many of the interior cabinets were painted in bold colors.

Triangular whatnot shelves are another common form.

A decoratively carved press for ironing out wrinkles in clothes (no heat required).

A baby cage and a boarded rocking toilet.

One of the hundreds of chests I've seen on my travels.

Delightful dugout chairs are as comfortable as they look.

APPENDIX 2

BOARDED TOOL CHEST

Excerpted from "The Anarchist's Design Book" (Lost Art Press).

Every household – even those devoid of a proper woodworker – needs a tool chest. On the day we closed on our first house (correction: our first slightly frightening shell) in Lexington, Kentucky, I bought a shiny red metal toolbox, a hammer, screwdrivers and a wooden miter box.

That metal box filled up within a month of work on the house and soon my tools took up two kitchen cabinets. A tool chest like the one shown here would have been a far superior choice, and it was in the range of my fresh-out-of-college skills (i.e. getting hammered and trying to nail something).

This chest is based on a lot of agricultural examples I've studied at antique stores, in private collections and at museums. It is designed to hold a kit of tools you need to maintain a household or farm, or to begin woodworking.

It is long enough to hold full-size handsaws – which are more common than the panel saws used by joiners – plus any planes, levels or bigger tools you might need. And the two sliding trays and any interior racks you might add can swallow all the little hand tools.

It's a great choice for a person who starts work on his or her house and makes the jump to furniture maker – the path that most North American woodworkers seem to take. It's also the chest I recommend new woodworkers build before tackling the full-size English tool chest presented in "The Anarchist's Tool Chest."

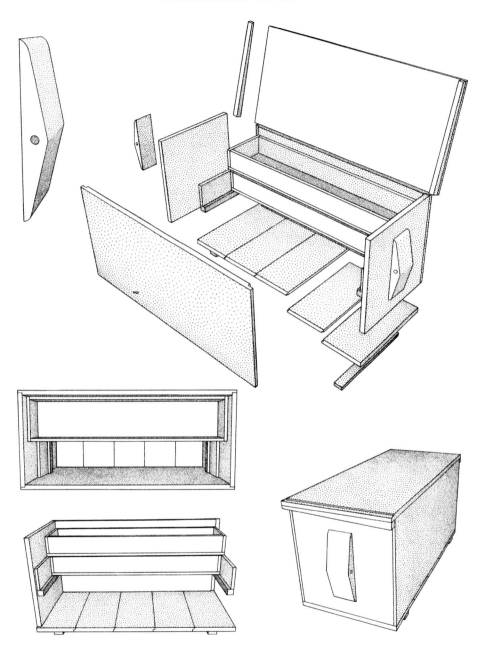

Illustrations by Briony Morrow-Cribbs

HOW IT'S BUILT

This chest is simple but, if made with care, stout enough to last a couple hundred years. The ends, front and back are rabbeted, glued and nailed – and the type of nail you choose is the key to the chest's long life.

The bottom is simply nailed to the underside of the carcase to make it easy to replace the bottom boards should they rot. As further protection against rot, there are two water-resistant "rot strips" screwed to the bottom to lift the chest off a wet floor.

The lid is a simple panel of wood with a batten screwed on at either end. The battens help keep the lid flat and also repel dust from penetrating your chest.

Inside the chest are two sliding trays – also nailed together – that slide on oak runners secured to the interior walls of the chest.

WOODS FOR BUILDING CHESTS

To make the chest easy to move, use the lightest-weight species you can find. My first choice: one of the white pines. Clear cedar, linden or cypress are almost as good. If you come up empty-handed, poplar will do. Tool chests get moved around. Even if you are a stay-at-home woodworker, you want a lightweight chest.

That said, there are a few bits and pieces of the chest that need to be resistant to water, wear and whacking. The rot strips take the most abuse. Consider using white oak or even something exotic (purpleheart or teak) if you have some scraps lying about.

The runners and the bottoms of the trays need to resist wear, so white oak is a good choice for these thin bits. And the battens that restrain the lid need to be straight and stout – oak again.

PREPARE THE PANELS

Dress the stock for the front, back and end panels. Cut the panels to width and length (see the cutting list at the end of the chapter) and remove any machine marks with a handplane.

Before cutting any joinery, mark the four panels using a cabinetmaker's triangle, a simple but effective marking system that will reduce the chance of an error during joinery or at assembly.

Now lay out the rabbets on the ends of the front and back panels. The 3/4"-wide x 3/8"-deep rabbets will strengthen the corner joint and assist you when you align your corners at assembly time.

This rabbet is cut across the grain of the panels, so you need to prevent the joint's shoulder from splintering as you cut it. A moving fillister plane has a nicker that knifes in a clean shoulder before the iron levers out the waste. So it's the best choice for this joint. (My second choice would be a straight rabbet plane that runs against a wooden fence.)

Two triangles. Mark the triangles on the top edges of your panels. Each triangle should point toward the front of the chest and be marked when the panel and its opposite part are placed together.

Extra step. Scribe in the width and depth of your rabbet with a cutting gauge. Use these lines to guide you as you fine-tune the setting of your moving fillister plane.

Even if you use a moving fillister, I recommend you first use a cutting gauge to define the waste. The cutting gauge's lines act as further insurance against splintering. Plus they will point out if your plane's fence or depth stop have moved during the operation.

Even the best moving fillister planes are fussy. The tool's iron and nicker need to be in perfect alignment and extend out from the body of the tool the tiniest amount so the plane will cut a square shoulder. The fence and depth stop can slip. And even if they don't slip, they won't save you from making a sloping, out-of-90° rabbet.

Making square rabbets requires practice and (until you are good) continuous inspection as you make the joint.

How you hold the tool is important. The fingers at the front of the tool should press the fence against the work. That hand's thumb should be in front of the mouth of the tool. The hand at the rear of the tool should push the plane only. If you grip the tool too tightly you will tilt it and cut a sloping rabbet.

Also important: where you put your head. It sounds odd, but you are much less likely to tilt the tool if your head is over the tool and you are looking at the

Head games. Get your head over the tool and use your hands to crowd the body of the tool against the work.

Verify. It's not a rabbet if it slopes down and the shoulder isn't 90°. That's a beveled moulding, and it is no good for joinery.

place where the tool's sidewall and the joint's shoulder meet.

Get in position. Start the tool at the far end of the work and pull it backward toward you. The nicker and your scribe line should be one and the same. If they aren't, you need to adjust the plane's fence.

If they are the same, then push the tool forward. When working across the grain you can take a thick shaving with ease. I usually start with a slightly thinner shaving on the first rabbet to make sure everything is in working order. After about four strokes, stop planing and check your work with a square. The floor of the rabbet needs to be 90° to the end of the board, and its shoulder should be perfectly vertical.

If things are out of whack, adjust your hands, and lean in or out slightly to correct the problem. Take two strokes to see how you did.

The next step is to nail the carcase together, so this will be your last opportunity to clean up any dings on the interior faces of the case.

NAIL THE CASE

The case is assembled with glue and nails. Considering all the end grain that is in these corner joints, you might not expect the box to be very strong. But if you apply the glue and nails in the correct way, it will outlive you.

Exposed joinery. You are going to see these nails every time you look at the chest, so I recommend spacing the five pilot holes at each corner with care.

As to the glue, I prefer hide glue for furniture in almost all cases, but if you have only yellow or white glue, it will be fine here. What's most important about the glue is that you use it to "size" the end grain in the joint before adding glue to the face-grain surfaces.

"Sizing" is simple. Paint a thin layer of glue on the end grain and let it sit for a minute, maybe two. This first application of glue will get sucked into the end grain and clog the wood's vessels. Then, when you apply the second coat of glue, the end grain will not be able to suck the glue away from the joint (that's what normally weakens a joint that uses end grain).

This procedure was developed by a glue scientist, but I've tested it in the shop. When these sized joints are intentionally broken, you see a lot of wood failure and little glue failure. That's a good thing.

The second factor is the nail you choose for the joint. You should use a tapered nail that has a significant head – either a cut nail, forged nail or a blacksmith-made wrought nail. These nails have a shank that tapers, and early 20th-century studies showed that these nails hold as much as 400 percent better than a same-size wire nail. That's because the nail's tapered shank acts like a wedge.

As to the size of nail, you can use a 4*d*, 5*d* or (in a pinch) 6*d* cut nail. The larger nails are more likely to split your work, but I'm going to show you how

Tape marks the stop. The pilot hole should stop short so the nail has to burrow its way into the material. Here I'm using a tapered drill bit for the pilot holes. It isn't strictly necessary, but it helps.

to get around that by clamping across the joint.

Lastly, you will strengthen the joint if you drill your pilot holes at alternating angles, kind of like dovetails. You don't want a lot of angle, just 5° or so. Mark out the locations of the five nails at each corner and get out the glue.

The most difficult part of using cut (or wrought) nails is drilling the correct pilot – both its diameter and length. The best way to approach the problem is to do some test joints in the same kind of material and get a feel for the correct diameter bit. With typical 4*d* and 6*d* nails I start with a 3/32" pilot hole and adjust up or down in size from there.

The pilot depth should be about two-thirds the length of the nail. If you make the pilot the full length (like with a screw), the nail's hold will be weak. The nail has to do some of the work.

The last thing to remember before driving the nails is that the tapering action of the nail should be parallel to the grain of the top board. If you apply the wedge across the grain, it's like splitting firewood. This confuses some people at first until they do it wrong. Then they never forget the rule.

Now it's time to put the box together. Begin by attaching the back to the ends.

Size the end grain of the end boards with a thin coat of glue and let it dry

A minute for strength. The thin coat of glue size on the end grain is an important component of a strong rabbeted butt joint.

for a minute. In the meantime, apply a thicker coat of glue in the rabbets on the back panel.

Place the back panel on the end panels and drill your pilot holes – don't forget to angle each hole slightly to increase the wedging action of the nails. If you are even the slightest bit worried about splitting (and I am always worried), put a bar clamp across the joint to reduce (greatly) the chance of the work busting apart.

Drive the nails and set the heads flush with the surface. Headed nails, such as clouts, roseheads and wrought-head nails, are not typically set below the surface of the work like a brad. Setting the head only increases the chance for splitting.

Affix the back panel. Flip the carcase over and repeat the process for the front panel. When the glue is dry, level your joints with a plane, including the top and bottom rim of the carcase.

BOTTOM BOARDS
The bottom boards are nailed to the bottom rim of the case. The individual boards should have some sort of edge joint to allow for seasonal movement. I used a tongue-and-groove joint; shiplaps would be another good choice.

Note that the grain of the bottom boards runs from front to back, not side to side. This is for strength.

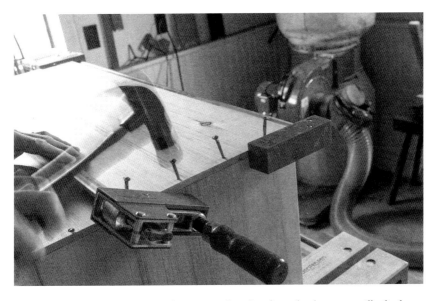

A clamp for safety. Clamping across the joint significantly reduces the chance you will split the top part of the joint or the board below. Note the alternating slopes of the nails – sometimes called "dovetailing" a nail.

Cut the edge joints on your bottom boards, then remove the machine marks. If you'd like to dress up the bottom boards, you can cut a small bead on the boards. If you are using a tongue-and-groove joint, cut the bead on the shoulder of the tongue section of the joint.

Now you can nail the bottom boards to the rim of the carcase using 6*d* clouts, roseheads or whatever headed nail you have on hand. Use the same pilot hole you used earlier for the carcase and apply a clamp across the carcase if you want to reduce the chance for splits.

After the bottom is on, true up the carcase all around to flush the bottom boards to the carcase.

THE ROT STRIPS

The last bit of work on the bottom is to affix the two rot strips to the underside of the bottom boards. There are three (at least) philosophies when it comes to rot strips. One philosophy is to make them from pine and affix them with iron nails. If these start to rot, they will fall off and you will know it's time to replace them.

The second philosophy is to make the rot strips from a water-resistant species and attach them with epoxy and brass screws. Then oil and wax them. These rot strips will refuse to rot or soak up water.

Special planes. While you can make a tongue-and-groove joint with plow and rabbet planes, it's much faster if you have a dedicated set of match planes or a metallic tongue-and-groove plane dedicated to the task.

A strong bead. Bead the shoulder of the tongue section of the joint. If you bead the groove section you will weaken the joint.

Nails all around. Don't glue the bottom boards, just use nails. I drive three nails into the ends of the carcase. Then I space the nails every 4" or 5" when nailing into the front and back of the carcase.

The third method? Skip the rot strips and screw casters to the chest.

All three methods protect the chest from moisture.

I had some teak scraps so I used those for the rot strips. After cutting them to size, I planed a small chamfer on the edges to make the chest easier to slide around on an uneven floor.

On this chest, I glued the rot strips on with epoxy and screwed them down with brass screws. A few coats of linseed oil on the teak and bottom boards will also help moisture from wicking into the carcase.

ADD THE CHEST LIFTS

The last bit of work is to make and attach the chest lifts on the ends. You can use metallic lifts or make your own using wood and rope.

There is no real advantage to either. Wooden lifts take time and effort to make, and they can break – I've seen it happen. Metallic chest lifts cost more to purchase, but they can be installed in a few minutes and are durable.

THE LID

The chest's lid is a simple flat panel with battens screwed to its ends. You can decorate the edges of the panel anyway you please – a thumbnail profile was a typical edge treatment.

Waterproof. Teak and epoxy will prevent water from migrating from the floor into your bottom boards.

To make the thumbnail profile, fetch your moving fillister plane. Use the same fence setting (a 3/4"-wide cut) as you did for the rabbet joinery. Adjust the depth stop so the plane takes a cut of about 1/8" deep.

Cut the profile on the ends first. Then rabbet the front edge of the lid. To complete the profile, use a block plane to round over the top lip of the panel.

Now affix the battens. On early chests, the battens were secured with clenched nails. This works really well, but it takes a little practice to get good at the operation. If you don't want to attempt clenched nails, the other option is to use wood screws in holes that are slightly elongated to allow for seasonal wood movement.

The first step is to shape the battens. At the least, ease the lower corners to make them nicer to handle. I sawed a bevel on the corners and cleaned up the cuts with a block plane.

Remove any machining marks and drill pilot holes and clearance holes for your wood screws. The clearance holes in the batten need to be slightly elongated parallel to the grain. This slight elongation allows the top to move without cracking.

Elongating the holes is simple, quick work. After drilling each clearance hole, put the bit back into the hole. While the bit is spinning, tip the drill forward then back about 10°. That's enough.

Your call. Chest lifts made from wood and rope, called "beckets," are one traditional choice. Iron lifts are another. There is no real functional advantage to either.

For decoration. It's OK if this rabbet slopes a bit. After cutting the rabbet on three sides, round over the sharp corner all around until it looks nice.

Screws that move. By elongating the clearance holes in the battens, the threads of the screw will stay tight in the lid (usually) without splitting.

Screw the battens to the lid. Then attach the lid to the carcase with hinges. Strap hinges look best here.

INTERIOR TRAYS

The two sliding tool trays hold all your small tools and grant you access to the large well below. The bottom tray sits on oak runners that are 5-1/2" above the floor of the chest. This space is critical because it allows you to put a typical bench plane on the floor of the chest with its sole flat on the bottom boards.

So the first task is to make a 5-1/2"-wide spacer so you can nail the lower runner in perfect position on either end of the carcase. Cut a scrap to this dimension and stand it on the floor of the chest. Place the lower runner on it. Glue and nail the runner to the wall of the carcase. Then glue and nail the remaining runner above it. Repeat at the other end.

With all the runners glued and nailed in, cut the bottom pieces for the trays to size and fit them to the inside of the carcase. It's easier to do this before you add the walls of the trays.

Permanent Jenga. The pine board shown at the bottom puts the lower runner in its correct position. After the first runner is in place, install the second runner on top of it. Then remove the spacer and repeat the process on the other end of the chest.

The trays are built a lot like the carcase with rabbets bonded with glue and headed nails. The rabbets on the end boards are 1/2" wide and 1/8" deep. The only significant difference between the trays and the carcase is that you want the bottom of the trays to poke out of the end of the assembled trays by 1/16". This slight proudness makes the trays simple to fit and ensures the nail heads won't rub against the interior walls of the chest and jam the trays.

You can attach the bottom to its tray with screws or nails. Just be sure to slightly elongate your clearance holes if you choose screws (nails will bend on their own without any further help).

A little beeswax on the trays and runners will help them slide, but that's

Shoot the bottom. After cutting the till bottom to a close size, shoot its ends until the bottom slides smoothly on its runners.

Familiar operation. The trays are assembled with the same joints and procedures as the carcase.

Slightly proud. Leaving the bottom end slightly proud of the tray solves a variety of potential problems.

really all the finish you need on the inside of the case.

On the outside, a few coats of a long-wearing paint is the typical choice for a tool chest. I used varnish alone on the lid, though that doesn't offer near the same protection as paint.

The rest is up to you. You can make racks for the inside walls to hold small tools. And there should be room to affix your handsaws to the inside of the lid.

Cutting list: Boarded Tool Chest

No.	Name	(inches) T	W	L
2	Front & back	3/4	15	33-1/2
2	Ends	3/4	15	14-1/4
	Bottom boards*	3/4	33-1/2	15
1	Lid	3/4	15-1/2	35
2	Lid battens	3/4	1	15-1/2
2	Rot strips	3/4	1-1/2	15
2	Lifts	1-1/2	3-1/4	10
2	Top tray, front & back	1/2	3	32
2	Top tray, ends	1/2	3	7
1	Top tray, bottom	1/2	7	32
2	Bottom tray, front & back	1/2	3	31
2	Bottom tray, ends	1/2	3	7
1	Bottom tray, bottom	1/2	7	31
2	Runners, lower tray	1	1	13-1/2
2	Runners, top tray	1/2	3-5/8	13-1/2

* Made up from multiple boards

ACKNOWLEDGMENTS

"The American Peasant" wouldn't exist if it weren't for Peter Follansbee, who introduced me to the work of Gyenes Tamás – my first step into the furniture traditions of Eastern Europe. That was followed by a long evening in a German farmhouse with psychedelic mushrooms and my friends Klaus Skrudland and Rudy Everts, who convinced me this book was possible.

John Cornall's exquisite taste in Carpathian furniture and his insights into the culture provided a good education in the furniture forms from the region. Many of the pieces in this book were inspired by antiques that Cornall imported, photographed and sold through John Cornall Antiques in Warwick, U.K. If you wish to continue your education in Eastern European folk furniture, follow his website and social media feeds.

Narayan Nayar, who is somehow an even better friend than a photographer, is responsible for the photos of the finished pieces.

As always, I am indebted to my fellow workers at Lost Art Press, who pick up my slack when I write a book, and they follow behind me cleaning up all the messes I make in writing and designing. Thanks to Megan Fitzpatrick, Kara Gebhart Uhl and John Hoffman for making my books possible and readable.

And finally, thanks to the subscribers of "The American Peasant" Substack. Their knowledge and critical feedback improved this book immeasurably. In particular, Brian Crawley, Daniel Traila and Péter Szalóki went out of their way to help with information and editing.

BIBLIOGRAPHY

Baud-Bovy, Daniel. *Peasant Art in Switzerland*. London: The Studio Ltd., 1924.

Csilléry, Klára K. *Hungarian Village Furniture*. Translated by Paul Aston. Budapest: Corvina Press, 1972.

Dzērvītis, Aleksandra. *Latvian Design*. Toronto: Latvian National Federation in Canada, 1973.

Fél, Edit, et al. *Hungarian Peasant Art*. Budapest: Corvina Press, 1958.

Harms, Mirja, et al. *Der Henndorfer Truhenfund*. Munich: Siegl, 2012.

Hoggard, Brian. *Magical House Protection*. Oxford: Berghahn Books, 2021.

Holme, Charles. *Peasant Art in Austria and Hungary*. London: The Studio Ltd., 1911.

---. *Peasant Art in Russia*. London: The Studio Ltd., 1912.

---. *Peasant Art in Sweden, Lapland and Iceland.* London: The Studio Ltd., 2015.

Longenecker, Martha. *Dowry.* San Diego: Mingei International Museum, 1999.

Ludwig, Allan I. *Graven Images.* Middletown, CT: Wesleyan University Press, 1966.

M Champion. *Medieval Graffiti: The Lost Voices of England's Churches.* London: Ebury Press, 2015.

Pageau, Matthieu. *The Language of Creation: Cosmic Symbolism in Genesis: A Commentary.* Columbia SC: 2018.

Perchyshyn, Natalie. *Ukrainian Design Book.* Minneapolis: Ukrainian Gift Shop Inc., 1986.

Roumanian Peasant Art. Bucharest: Luceafarul, 1940.

Tamás, Gyenes. *Áscolt Ládák Titkai.* Budapest: self published, 2011.